THE MASTER LANDSCAPE ARCHITECT SERIES

BELT COLLINS

BELT COLLINS

First published in Australia in 2003
by The Images Publishing Group Pty Ltd
ABN 89 059 734 431
6 Bastow Place, Mulgrave, Victoria, 3170, Australia
Telephone (61 3) 9561 5544 Facsimile (61 3) 9561 4860
Email: books@images.com.au
Website: www.imagespublishinggroup.com

National Library of Australia
Cataloguing-in-Publication data

Belt Collins.

Includes index.
ISBN 1 876907 31 2.

1. Belt Collins Hawaii (Firm). 2. Landscape architectural firms –
Hawaii. 3. Landscape architecture – Hawaii. 4. Landscape
architects – Hawaii. I. Title. (Series: Master landscape architect
series).

712.09969

Edited by Fiona Gruber
Designed by The Graphic Image Studio Pty Ltd, Mulgrave, Australia
Film by Ocean Graphic Company Limited
Printed by Max Production Printing & Book-binding Limited

IMAGES has included on its website a page for special notices in
relation to this and our other publications. Please visit this site:
www.imagespublishinggroup.com

CONTENTS

Belt Collins

INTRODUCTION

It is said that a multi-disciplinary firm such as Belt Collins serves three masters: the *land* with all its diversity in form, culture and history; the *owners* and their need for a contribution to the environment as well as economic needs; and certainly the *users* who have the final appraisal of whether a project works well or not.

During its fifty years of creating development projects–from barren lava fields along the Kohala Coast on the Big Island of Hawai'i to the lush, tropical jungles of Bali and thousands of places in between–Belt Collins, with its talented landscape architects, environmental specialists, physical planners and civil engineers, has served all three masters continuously with great skill.

Prominent among those skills is an ability to transform the land with a practiced eye toward integrating the natural with the man-made. For the professionals at Belt Collins, it is not enough to simply change a land mass in its original form for the satisfaction of a few; it is much more important to bring into being a piece of work that enhances what was there before while creating usefulness and beauty for many. As an example, by careful planning, via the Ayers Rock Destination Plan in Australia, the firm was able to unlock a greater appreciation of the Aboriginal Tribes that inhabit the area.

There are hundreds of examples where Belt Collins professionals incorporated the designs, using the local history and culture of the area, into their work. One is the Champs de Bataille golf course in France. The design called for integrating the existing formal French garden and historic chateau into the overall design so that they became a part of the first 18 holes.

Consider, too, that Belt Collins works among some of the world's most interesting cultures. It takes a richness of understanding to design projects that assimilate the Chamoro in Guam, the Chinese in Hainan, the Aborigines in Australia and the tremendous mix of cultures in Hawai'i–just to mention a few of the various peoples encompassed by the firm's wide-ranging work.

A diversity of people among its many worldwide projects, yes, but also think of the oftentimes totally dissimilar codes and regulations faced by the many Belt Collins professionals as they design and build a hotel landscape project in Malaysia, a resort in Indonesia, and a whole new town in China.

Integration and teamwork are very important concepts for Belt Collins as they design large-scale projects. What that means is a coordinated process involving all the disciplines. It starts with the master planners as the team leaders whose final work only appears on paper. In all cases the environmental consultants are members of the team and quietly do their work, which, if successful, is never seen. Then the firm's civil engineers become the team leaders and go to work artfully engineering the roads and infrastructure most of which, if well done, is hidden from view.

Finally, the landscape architects become the team leaders and create the final environment that is seen and experienced. Throughout the entire process all the disciplines are involved as a team. The end result, as Belt Collins' clients have found, is a property that works perfectly, pleasing both owners and users.

1 Ayers Rock Destination Plan
   Yulara, Australia
2 Bali Golf & Country Club
   Nusa Dua, Bali, Indonesia
3 Safari Park & Casino
   Nairobi, Kenya

This is one of the many reasons that time and again the same owner has retained the firm as a particular large-scale project has progressed over the years. One of the best examples of this long-term owner satisfaction started with an airplane ride and picnic on a remote beach on the Big Island of Hawai'i. In the mid-'60s Laurance Rockefeller and his team, along with selected governmental officials and other interested parties, were searching for a Hawai'i property that might be developed under the RockResorts brand.

Walter Collins was a leader in the effort among the passengers who flew over the uninhabited, partially barren lava of the Kohala Coast on that long-ago day. From the time Rockefeller and his party arrived on the remote and beautiful beach until today, Belt Collins has created a continuity of design for the famed Mauna Kea Resort that spans more than a quarter century. In fact, the firm's work for Mauna Kea has set destination resort standards for projects around the world.

Another example of continuity of service is the work the firm has done for the Kuok family and their group of Shangri-La hotels throughout the Pacific. It started with the Shangri-La in Singapore and has progressed from there through 28 other properties from the Philippines, to China, Hong Kong and beyond.

Because of its long history and worldwide reputation for excellence, Belt Collins became one of the first major design firms to do the seminal, integrated work that led to the creation of major resorts, especially in Hawai'i, but also in other locales such as Australia, American and Western Samoa, Sri Lanka, Fiji, Malaysia, Guam and Taiwan. In the last, a Visitor Destination Study identified destination areas for that island, taking into consideration elements such as air transportation from neighboring regions to Taiwan.

Another example is the firm's planning and engineering involvement with the West Hawai'i Highway Corridor Study in 1968, which called for a new coastal highway. Once built, the Queen Ka'ahumanu Highway has served as the vital link between six major destination resorts along the Kohala Coast, the airport and the seaside town of Kailua-Kona. The firm also performed the engineering design for the Lalamilo Water System that made possible the development of the Mauna Lani Resort and others along the Kohala Coast. Its work didn't stop there. Belt Collins has provided master and site planning, civil engineering, environmental consulting, landscape architecture and golf course design in total or in part for all six majors resorts up and down the Kohala Coast.

While serving the hospitality industry has been a long-term success for Belt Collins, the firm and its professionals have brought their considerable skills to many other types of projects, both public and private. Consider the transformation of Sentosa Island for the government of Singapore from a derelict British military base fronting the South China Sea into a proud recreational development with a hotel, shops, offices and housing.

The span of work by Belt Collins' many professionals is difficult to categorize simply. The diversity of projects includes historic hotels in Singapore, Cambodia and Honolulu; cultural parks in Malaysia, Indonesia and Kenya; entertainment venues in Australia, Hawai'i and the Philippines; sports and recreation facilities in all the places mentioned so far, as well as France, Thailand and Hong Kong; major resorts and hotels in these places, plus Egypt, Israel and India; and residential and urban communities all over the world. These are only the beginning.

1 Dynasty Court
  Shenzhen, China
2 Rainbow Run
  Redmond, Washington, USA
3 Champs de Bataille Golf Course
  Le Neubourg, Normandy, France

1   2   3

Belt Collins has had an impact in many different ways around the Pacific. One of the more interesting is summed up in a story about Walter Collins travelling with Pete Wimberly in the mid-1960s. One of their stops was in Singapore where they met with the then Prime Minister Lee Kwan Yew and other government officials. At the conclusion of the meeting, Lee Kwan Yew asked Walter, 'what would you do to enhance the environment of Singapore as a tourist destination?' Walter's reply, 'plant trees!'

For anyone who has visited Singapore during the last quarter of the 20th century, it is fair to say, in the words of George Lipp, Market and Financial Specialist with the Shangri-La Group, 'that Singapore now has more trees than most national forests'. Lee Kwan Yew, who was Prime Minister of Singapore between 1953 and 1990, still serves as a senior minister in its parliament.

This book can only include a fraction of the projects Belt Collins has designed. The intention of this book is to give the reader and viewer a taste of the firm's award-winning work.

One last word in this introduction is a must, and it has to do with Belt Collins' legion of professionals who reflect the diversity in age, gender, training and ethnicity of the many offices where the firm works. They are talented to be sure. They work as a team, not just in thought, but also in spirit. Many have been with the firm for a quarter century and more, making their mark over and over again. Their work has been showered with awards from the most prestigious organizations in the world. They are the soul of the firm. This book is, in small measure, a tribute to their award-winning efforts.

One of the most recognized and popular vacation destination areas in the world was never planned as a resort. Rather, its great attributes have always made it a natural recreational oasis. It is more a matter of making man's structures fit in with the beauty of its beaches, the ocean and the superb climate.

That Waikiki still works splendidly today is due in part to the continuing work Belt Collins has performed in the area over the past 50 years. Consider that, of the six million plus visitors who come to Hawai'i annually, five million stay and play in Waikiki.

In the early days most of Waikiki was given over to duck ponds, banana patches and rice paddies, with a few dwellings along the beach for Hawaiian royalty. Then the grand hotel, The Moana, was built shortly after the turn of the 20th century. The Royal Hawaiian Hotel followed it about 25 years later.

During these years Waikiki was a playground and place of respite for Hawaiian royalty and for the wealthy who had the time and resources to travel by ship to the islands. During this time the government and private interests had focused on the resort potential for the whole area. So in 1920 work began on the 1.5-mile canal known as the Ala Wai that cleaned up all the low-lying land.

For many years a smattering of visitors came to the two hotels on the beach; cottages were built here and there on the reclaimed land, and a few local surfers enjoyed the gentle waves. In the early '50s, however, the advent of jet travel from the West Coast meant that Waikiki became accessible to the average tourist.

That started a boom that continues to this day. It was around this time that Belt Collins was formed as a land planning and engineering firm. In a way, one could say that modern Waikiki and the firm started out together.

Because of the diversity of interest groups within the private and public sectors, no comprehensive plan has ever been agreed on, even though a master plan for all of Waikiki has been promoted and discussed for many years. Waikiki has been a huge success, nonetheless, due in part to the significant work Belt Collins has provided in the way of public and private amenities from one end of Waikiki to the other for over a 50-year span.

Work for the public sector has ranged from urban design and environmental studies, engineering infrastructure design, beach reclamation and canal dredging, to overall design for parks, a golf course, beach promenade, zoo and streetscapes. For the private sector, Belt Collins has performed extensive landscape work for a number of hotels and shopping/retail complexes. In addition, the firm has assisted a major land trust with land-related issues in Waikiki since 1984.

Opposite:
Waikiki with Diamond Head in the background

WAIKIKI: ONE OF THE WORLD'S GREAT RESORTS

THE ROYAL HAWAIIAN
Honolulu, Hawai'i, USA

Client
*Helumoa Land Co. and
Gulstrom/Kosko, Sheraton*

An excellent example of Belt Collins' efforts in Waikiki is the firm's work for the fabled 'Pink Palace', The Royal Hawaiian.

When the firm was engaged to redesign and renovate the landscape for the historic hotel, it set three goals: first, to emphasize the original scale and design of three existing gardens; second, to screen out, as much as possible, the surrounding buildings with appropriate plant material; and third, to redesign the landscaped areas in such a way that they could be used for multiple purposes, given the value of the land where the hotel sits.

Because many of the mature coconut trees on the hotel grounds were planted by Hawaiian royalty, the plan called for protecting them wherever possible. Lawns, pathways and beds of groundcover were redefined to create bold and interesting shapes when seen from the upper floors as well as by guests strolling the grounds.

The end result is that guests from other Waikiki hotels seek out this restful green space as a place to relax and recall the grace and splendor of an earlier era in Hawai'i.

2

Opposite:
The 'Pink Palace' now surrounded by high-rise hotels.
2 The Royal looking toward the ocean.
3 Guests from other hotels are attracted to the Royal's tropical oasis in the heart of Waikiki.

3

5

6

4&5 Mature coconut trees, originally planted by
Hawaiian royalty, were preserved during
garden renovation.
6 In most cases the hotel does not rise above
the height of the coconut trees.
7 The Royal has a special niche in Waikiki.
8&9 The garden design creates an enclave in the
midst of bustling Waikiki.

7

8

9

1

2

ROYAL HAWAIIAN SHOPPING CENTER

Honolulu, Hawai'i, USA

Client
Helumoa Land Co.

3

4

The owners of the Royal Hawaiian Shopping Center engaged Belt Collins to create a thoroughly Hawaiian landscape setting for the two-block-long center, recognized as the premier shopping area of Waikiki's famed Kalakaua Avenue.

Belt Collins' master plan and engineering studies called for setting the sidewalk back closer to the shopping center buildings. That allowed the creation of a garden setback and safety zone adjacent to the street. The result has been an enhanced shopping experience for the thousands of pedestrians on Kalakaua Avenue and beautification of the streetscape along the center's frontage. At the time it was conceived, this concept was quite revolutionary.

This Royal Hawaiian Shopping Center landscape design was, in many ways, the catalyst for the City and County of Honolulu to ask the Belt Collins/Fox Hawaii team to prepare and implement what became the two-mile-long Kalakaua Avenue Beautification Project.

Since shoppers enter the center from both Kalakaua Avenue and the historic gardens of the Royal Hawaiian Hotel, it means that the center has no back. The firm's landscape architects worked to integrate the hotel's restful gardens with the commerce of the center by creating a series of pathways and indoor/outdoor restaurant spaces facing the interior gardens.

Because of the length and height of the center, it contains two major courtyards. For these, Belt Collins created softening landscapes by planting trees and cascading plant material down the four stories of the center. In the process, a rare Aki tree was saved from demolition by moving it (at great expense) just a few feet into one of the interior courtyards. This was a highly publicized decision that turned out to be a win for both the developers and the historic preservationists.

1　Tropical planting and a waterfall draw pedestrians to the center.
2　Placing the sidewalk back from the street allowed a thoroughly Hawaiian landscape along Kalakaua Avenue.
3　The famed Aki tree as it looks today among mature planting.
4　Aki tree just after it was moved a few feet to become part of the landscape plan.

1 The Hyatt's Great Hall is a block-long open-air
   atrium that functions as a tropical town square.
2 Twin 40-story towers of the Hyatt Regency
   Waikiki span an entire block.

HYATT REGENCY WAIKIKI

Honolulu, Hawai'i, USA

Client
Hemmeter Investments

The 40-story twin-tower Hyatt Regency Waikiki was the first true high-rise hotel built on Kalakaua Avenue. To bring together the two towers, architects Wimberly Allison Tong & Goo designed a Great Hall which has been described as a block-long, open-air atrium that functions like a tropical town square.

As the resort's activity center, the Great Hall serves many functions: the arrival and registration point, a casual meeting spot, a place for pageantry, and a place for dining and shopping in more than 70 retail stores and restaurants.

Belt Collins designed extensive landscaping for the Great Hall which includes three waterfalls. Luxuriant tropical foliage in the form of full-sized palm trees and colorful shrubbery creates inviting nooks and crannies. On festive occasions, choirs sing from the open stairways as visitors dine in the landscaped courtyard café. A typical resort afternoon or evening finds Hawaiian music groups entertaining in this delightful space.

2

3

4

5

6

3 Sunlight washes the open-air interior.
4&5 Tropical foliage creates inviting nooks and crannies in the Great Hall.
6 View from upper balcony to outdoor dining area.
7&8 Three waterfalls enhance the tropical town square concept.

7

8

1

3

2

1 Initial work on one of the largest landfill projects in the Pacific.
2 The result was one of the first man-made beaches in the Pacific.
3 Ala Moana Park and Magic Island looking toward Diamond Head.
4 The park provides recreation for millions of residents and visitors annually.
5 Ala Moana Beach is an urban strip of white sand beach over a half mile long.
6 Walkers, runners and bicyclists are major users of the park.

4

ALA MOANA PARK/ MAGIC ISLAND

Honolulu, Hawai'i, USA

Client
*City and County of Honolulu,
Department of Parks and Recreation*

*State of Hawai'i, Department of Land
and Natural Resources, State Parks
Division*

5

6

Like many growing urban areas, in its early days Honolulu saw some dramatic changes in its shoreline. Commerce and health played a big part in re-shaping the area from downtown through Waikiki.

Midway between those areas was a large empty parcel of mostly duck ponds that a private company saw as having great potential. Thus Hawaiian Dredging began a long-range project in 1927 that eventually created one of the world's most successful shopping centers (commonly called just Ala Moana) and today's much-used Ala Moana Beach Park. Together they represent one of the largest landfill projects in the Pacific.

In 1961, Belt Collins presented a comprehensive engineering program for what was called the Ala Moana Reef Plan to the State Department of Land and Natural Resources. What was unusual about this plan was that it showed the development for three pieces of land that did not yet exist.

The engineering idea was to expand the recreational aspects of Ala Moana Beach Park by creating an offshore reef, a large land extension to be known as Magic Island and another peninsula at the Kewalo Basin. One of the recommendations of the plan was to extend Waikiki by selectively placing hotels on Magic Island.

In the end, the recreational uses won out, and while Magic Island (it is not really an island) was built, the offshore reef and the Kewalo peninsula were not. This was, however, the first successful man-made beach in the Pacific of substantial size. The engineering method that proved to create a stable sand level has been used over and over as a guide for many other beaches of this type.

The result is that Waikiki is now anchored on its northern end by a very sizable recreational area where residents and visitors alike can swim, surf, sunbathe, picnic, ride bikes, jog, rollerblade and just kick back and relax.

Other Significant Waikiki Design Work by Belt Collins:

Kalakaua Avenue Beautification, Honolulu, Hawai'i, USA

2100 Kalakaua, Honolulu, Hawai'i, USA

Hawaii Prince Hotel, Honolulu, Hawai'i, USA

Outrigger Canoe Club, Honolulu, Hawai'i, USA

Hale Koa Hotel, Honolulu, Hawai'i, USA

Ilikai Hotel, Honolulu, Hawai'i, USA

Honolulu Zoo, Honolulu, Hawai'i, USA

1

2

3

4

5

6

1 Kalakaua Avenue before Belt Collins engineers, planners and landscape architects worked to bury all utilities to create a place of tropical beauty.

2 After photo of the completed Kalakaua Beautification Project.

3&4 By placing the sidewalk back from the street in certain places, a thoroughly Hawaiian landscape was created along the major shopping center front.

5 Members and guests enter Outrigger Canoe Club under a vine-covered arbor and tropical planting.

6 The twin towers of the Hawaii Prince Hotel nestle among a tropical landscape with the Ala Wai Yacht Basin in the foreground.

7

8

9

10

11

12

13

7 Pool at the Hale Koa Hotel.
8 Hale Koa Hotel walkways.
9 Night mood shot of new 2100 Kalakaua shopping
   plaza in Waikiki.
10 Detail of fountain at 2100 Kalakaua.
11 Guest deck with pools, water feature and landscape at
   Ilikai Hotel.
12&13 Kids and their parents are treated to an African
   savannah at the Honolulu Zoo in Waikiki.

The West Coast of the Island of Hawai'i was once one of the most populated areas of the Hawaiian island chain.

Native Hawaiians launched their canoes from white crescent-shaped beaches. Ancient villages dotted the calm shore where ingenious fishponds stored the bounty of the sea. At mid-elevation on the vast lava slopes of Mauna Loa and Hualalai volcanoes were agricultural settlements, surrounded by very long stonewalls, growing crops for all. Higher in the mountains were artisans who made crude stone implements used by their brethren, in part, to carve expressive petroglyphs near the shore.

For hundreds of years early Hawaiians made their way along the shoreline either by outrigger canoe or on foot, going from Hawi in the north to Ho'okena in the south. Trails also connected the mountains with the sea. Until the 1950s these historic paths were the only access to the entire area, and they have been preserved to this day.

Kamehameha I, the great warrior who unified the islands into one kingdom (except the island of Kaua'i) in the 1700s, was born in the Kohala District of the Big Island. Contact with the outside world was first made along this coast at Kealakekua Bay, when Captain James Cook landed in 1778. A second significant landing took place when Christian missionaries from New England landed in the area in 1820.

These factors and more make the Kohala Coast one of the most intriguing visitor destination areas in the world.

This was a point made clear in 1960 when the Hawai'i state government published the Visitor Destination Area Study, of which Belt Collins was a key participant. That study's main conclusion was that Hawai'i's infant tourism industry would grow substantially over the years, and that to assure success in the future, resort destinations would need to be developed beyond Waikiki in special places on the neighbor islands. This proposition seems simple now in retrospect, but at the time it signaled a dramatic turn for Hawai'i's infant visitor industry.

Opposite:
Mauna Lani Resort

THE KOHALA COAST OF HAWAI'I

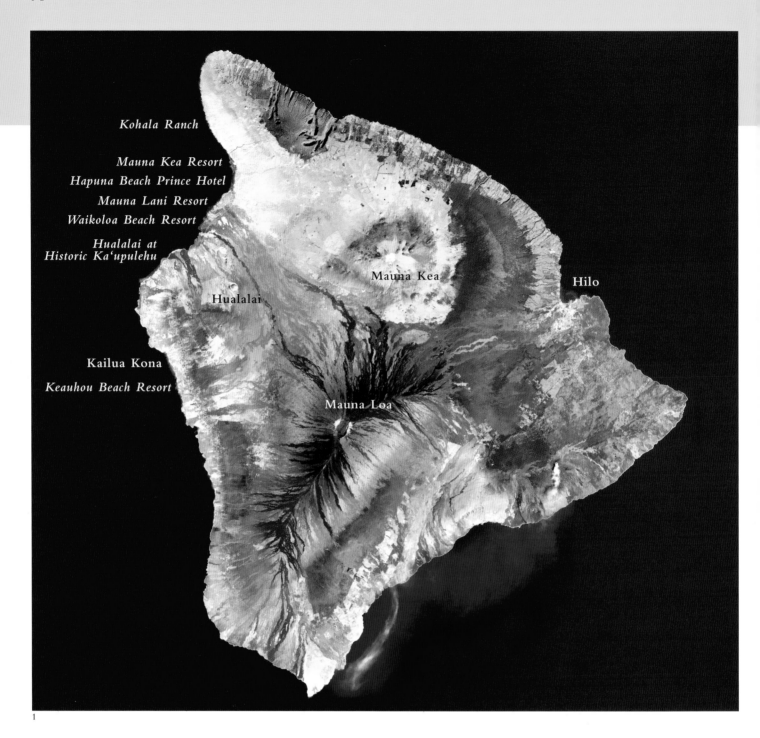

Kohala Ranch

Mauna Kea Resort
Hapuna Beach Prince Hotel
Mauna Lani Resort
Waikoloa Beach Resort

Hualalai at
Historic Ka'upulehu

Mauna Kea

Hualalai

Hilo

Kailua Kona

Keauhou Beach Resort

Mauna Loa

1

In the latter part of 1962, Belt Collins, with others, acted on the results of the Visitor Destination Study when they convinced environmentalist and businessman/resort developer Laurance Rockefeller to fly over selected areas of the Kohala Coast.

As he studied the entire area, Rockefeller became especially interested in two factors. Over the years the early Hawaiian settlements had died out, and the land he and his party saw had become a vast area of bare lava rock, sparse haole koa shrubs and sprouts of pili grass. The ancient trails were uncovered with difficulty, and most access to the still lovely beaches and fishing areas was only by rough jeep trail. There were no roads per se.

Given the history of the area, Rockefeller wanted to be as environmentally sensitive as possible, and to that end he spent more than a year with Belt Collins, studying and planning which plant life was best suited to the area.

The second factor was the coming demise of the sugar industry. Rockefeller supported the State government's desire to create jobs to replace those lost to agriculture.

Mr. Rockefeller was clearly a visionary to see the potential of a world-class resort nestled next to Kauna'oa Beach those many years ago. Matched with the vision of Belt Collins' master plan for the property, what was created at Mauna Kea Beach Resort has set enduring standards for quality development around the world.

2

1 Belt Collins' major projects on the Kohala Coast of the
  Big Island of Hawai'i.
2 Hualalai Resort.

1

1 A portion of the Kohala Coast before any development.
Below:
     An aerial view of the 3,800-acre Mauna Kea Resort for
     which Belt Collins provided master planning, site planning,
     landscape architecture and civil engineering, starting in
     1962 and continuing today.
3 View of the ocean and golf course including the Mauna
     Lani Villas.
4 Aerial view of the very first stages of the resort
     development.

MAUNA KEA RESORT

Kohala, Hawai'i, USA

Client
Olohana Corporation

*Palmer Course Design Company has always
enjoyed and respected working with Belt Collins...
they are first rate and first class professionals.*

Arnold Palmer

3

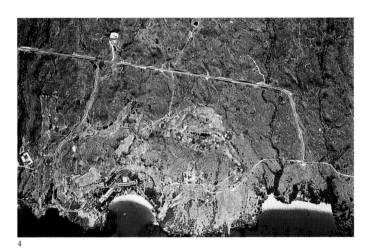

4

The architectural firm of Skidmore Owings & Merrill designed the first phase, and Wimberly Allison Tong & Goo the second phase of the award-winning Mauna Kea Beach Hotel. The resort is one of many long-term client relationships Belt Collins has enjoyed over the years, even as the resort has gone through several owners. The firm's contributions helped create Mauna Kea, which is a 3,850-acre self-contained luxury resort, residential and recreation community that has been developed in increments since 1962.

To demonstrate the depth of respect **Laurance Rockefeller** held for the work of Belt Collins, he had installed on the property a bronze plaque that reads:

Dedicated to the Memory of Walter Kittredge Collins, Whose Heart and Hand Enhanced the Beauty Here. Laurance S. Rockefeller, July 4, 1975.

The firm has provided master planning, site planning, landscape design and civil engineering, as the resort has progressed from the original hotel through other structural and recreational development. Part of Belt Collins' continuing work for Mauna Kea involved the master planning for the Fairway Homes North and South, which are single-family residential communities. The firm's work included actual siting for each house on an individual lot, so that ocean views were maintained. The Bluffs are duplexes for which Belt Collins also provided master planning and landscape design.

In each phase, the overall theme has been one of simplicity. Engineers worked with the planners and landscape architects to create narrow roadways and hidden infrastructure, creating a clean profile that had not been seen before.

The firm worked with Robert Trent Jones, Sr. on the original golf course, and with Arnold Palmer on the second course. Mauna Kea Resort was awarded an Urban Land Institute Award for Excellence for large-scale recreational development in 1987. The resort also includes a tennis complex, a second hotel called the Hapuna Beach Prince Hotel and single-family luxury residential developments.

5 Beautiful beaches and golf courses provide ample recreation.
Below:
    Gentle surf adds to the resort's allure.

5

Arnold Palmer said of Belt Collins,

Palmer Course Design Company has always enjoyed and respected working with Belt Collins. We have been working with Jim Bell and his gang for more than twenty years. They are first rate and first class professionals.

As Mauna Kea Resort grew and prospered, it was evident that infrastructure was needed if the entire Kohala Coast was going to be developed further. Jeep trails would no longer suffice; water was a key issue in this huge dry area; and electricity was needed close to the resorts.

Belt Collins provided engineering studies and plans in all these critical areas. The 1968 West Hawaii Highway Corridor Study, which won a national Consulting Engineers Award, resulted in today's Queen Ka'ahumanu Highway that over its 35 miles smoothly connects Kawaihae with Kailua-Kona and the resorts in

between. The firm's work in this area took into consideration the history and culture of the area, the various landowners and uses and the growth potential for the entire Kohala Coast.

Again taking the environmentally sensitive approach, Rockefeller worked with Belt Collins and the County of Hawai'i on an engineering study to locate the major power lines (that could have been run right alongside Queen Ka'ahumanu Highway) 1,500 feet mauka (towards the mountains) to preserve view planes all along the roadway.

The Lalamilo Water System Study prepared by Belt Collins in 1980, perhaps the most critical engineering study in the whole area, set out a plan to bring water from deep wells at upper elevations to the burgeoning Kohala Coast resorts.

This study and the subsequent water brought by the system made it possible for the growth that today has resulted in five world-class destination resorts along the Kohala Coast. For each of these

resorts Belt Collins has provided all or portions of master planning, civil engineering, golf course design and landscape architecture.

From that early day in 1962 with Laurance Rockefeller until today, the Kohala Coast continues to be an area of great beauty. It has also been turned into a great economic engine as well. The area from Mauna Kea to Hualalai now offers 4,300 hotel rooms and condominiums.

The resorts and hotels along the coast employ some 7,000 people with a payroll just under $170 million. The taxes generated are substantial: nearly $9 million in property tax for the county, and $40 million in general excise tax for the state. Included in the $2.5 billion that Kohala Coast resorts have invested are water resources, wastewater treatment plants, parks, child-care facilities, schools and a fire station.

7

A further acknowledgement of the work of Belt Collins was provided by **Harry Mullikin**, former Chairman and CEO of Westin Hotels (one of the owners of the Mauna Kea Beach Hotel) who said,

When told of a neighbor's nephew moving to Honolulu to join a landscape architectural company called Belt Collins, I said, 'Belt Collins is not a company–it's an institution!' During my time as chairman, we worked with Belt Collins on many of Westin's most notable properties in the Hawaiian Islands and elsewhere in the Pacific Rim countries. Their team of professionals always seemed to find the most creative and efficient design solutions for our development projects.

7   Guests stroll the hotel's tropical gardens.
8   Carefully selected art pieces grace the hotel's exterior and interior.
9   Looking north with the Hapuna Beach Prince Hotel in the foreground and Mauna Kea Beach Hotel in the background.
10 Present day Mauna Kea Beach Hotel with 13,000-foot Mauna Kea in the background right.

8

9

10

1

1 Mauna Lani Resort before any development.
2 Mauna Lani is a 3,200-acre destination resort master planned by Belt Collins, which also provided civil engineering, landscape architecture, golf course design and environmental consulting.
3 Mauna Lani entry sign.
4 Unique arrow shape allows 90 percent of the rooms to enjoy ocean views.
5 The landscaping provides an oasis in the middle of barren lava.

2

MAUNA LANI RESORT
Kohala, Hawai'i, USA

Client
Mauna Lani Resort

This 3,200-acre resort offers two carriage-trade hotels, two 18-hole championship golf courses, a racquet club, beach club and several residential neighborhoods including luxury condominiums.

The Francis H. I'i Brown Golf Course opened in 1981, followed in 1983 by the Mauna Lani Bay Hotel and Bungalows designed by Killingsworth and Brady. Surrounded by tropical gardens, the hotel's unique arrow shape allows ocean views for 90 percent of its 350 rooms. In 1990 a 539-room hotel now known as The Fairmont Orchid, Hawai'i, designed by Wimberly Allison Tong & Goo, opened along with the resort's second 18-hole golf course.

Belt Collins provided master planning, civil engineering, landscape architecture and environmental consulting for the entire resort. The Mauna Lani Golf Course, which has been acclaimed as translating art into landscape, was also engineered and designed by Belt Collins and built by Homer Flint. This resort is one of the best examples of the integration of the firm's disciplines which all came together here to work as an innovative team, including the engineering work that created beaches for both the Mauna Lani Beach Club and The Orchid.

The resort remains a client of the firm today.

3

4

5

6

7

8

9

6&9 Hotel lobby carries exterior garden concept inside.
7 Aerial view of Mauna Lani resort complex, which includes two carriage trade hotels, two championship golf courses, a racquet club, beach club and several residential neighborhoods.
8 The Beach Bungalows have proved very popular.
10 Natural anchialine ponds were preserved and integrated into the overall landscape design.

10

1

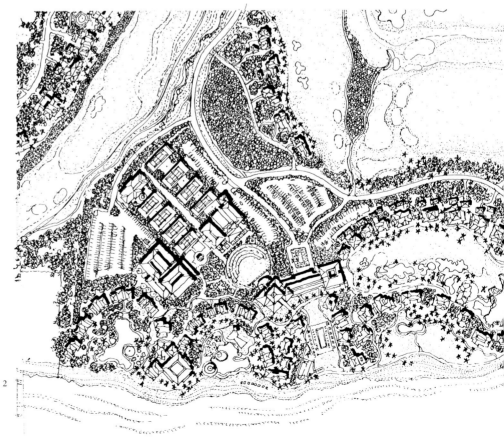

2

HUALALAI RESORT

Ka'upulehu, Hawai'i, USA

Client
Hualalai Resort

3

The latest in this string of jeweled resorts on the Kohala Coast is Hualalai Resort at Historic Ka'upulehu, with the Four Seasons Resort designed by Hill Glazier Architects. The first step in the resort process was an 18-hole championship course designed by Jack Nicklaus, built on bare, black lava. This was done in 1995 to accommodate the Senior PGA Tour's MasterCard Championship. In 1999, the resort was given the Award of Excellence by the Urban Land Institute.

In further testament to Belt Collins' talents in golf course design, engineering and landscape design work **Jack Nicklaus** said

My team and I have worked with Belt Collins on quite a few projects throughout the Pacific Rim, and on each occasion they have produced quality work and have been a pleasure to work with. If you simply look at the projects we did together in Hawai'i—be it Hualalai or Kauai Lagoons or Manele—each one has received national and international recognition. That is a reflection of what happens when you assemble a good team, and Belt Collins was a key part of each of those teams.

We at Nicklaus wish Belt Collins the best of luck, and hopefully, we'll have the opportunity to work together again in the next 50 years.

The Four Seasons Hotel Hualalai opened in 1996 as an upscale property offering a wide range of amenities. The master plan made way for preservation of ancient anchialine pools near the shoreline as well as an ancient trail at the water's edge.

Located in the ancient Ka'upulehu area at the base of the old lava flow from Hualalai Mountain, the hotel has provided a Hawaiian Cultural Center with displays of cultural artifacts. Belt Collins continues to provide engineering, planning and landscape architecture for the Hualalai Resort as it moves forward with its continuing development phases.

1 Bird's eye view of the resort shortly after it opened.
2 Vignette of Master Plan for hotel and 18th hole.
3 The resort includes two championship golf courses, five pools including a lap pool and natural lava pool for snorkeling, eight tennis courts, a sports club and spa, and several hundred residences.

4

4 White sand beach on the right and ancient anchialine ponds beyond.

5 The bold simplicity of the wili wili tree and a'a lava rock monument distinguish the Hualalai entry sign.

6 The Jack Nicklaus designed golf course was built on bare lava with Belt Collins providing civil engineering and landscape architecture.

7 Restored pond where once Hawaiian kings swam is now enjoyed by hotel guests.

8 Condominiums adjacent to the golf course have proven very popular.

9 Water is a critical component to the resort and two water wells developed by Belt Collins engineers are visible in this aerial photo.

5

6

If you simply look at the projects we did together in Hawai'i—be it Hualalai or Kauai Lagoons or Manele— each one has received national and international recognition.

Jack Nicklaus

7

8

9

1 Waikoloa Beach Marriott, an Outrigger Resort.
Below:
   The Hilton is a giant play land that includes a 1,200-room hotel, monorail, waterway with gondolas and special dolphin program.
3 Waikoloa Beach Resort, for which Belt Collins provided master planning, civil engineering, environmental consulting and landscape architecture, is 1,350 acres with two world-class hotels, three luxury condominiums, two championship golf courses and a shopping center.

WAIKOLOA BEACH RESORT

Kohala, Hawai'i, USA

Client
Waikoloa Land Company

This resort comprises 1,350 acres with two hotels, three luxury condominiums, 75,000 square feet of retail space and two championship golf courses. In the early years Belt Collins provided master planning, civil engineering and landscape architecture for the resort, which remains a client today.

The first Waikoloa hotel opened in 1981 along with the 18-hole Beach Golf Course. Now known as the Waikoloa Beach Marriott, an Outrigger Resort, this newly renovated 545-room property overlooks historic fishponds and the curve of white sand beach along Anaeho'omalu Bay. A second hotel, the 1,240-room Hilton Waikoloa Village opened in 1988. Its sheer size, its monorail, its waterway with gondolas and its special dolphin program boggle the minds of first time visitors. The second championship golf course, The King's Course, opened in 1990.

3

4

5

6

7

8

4&5 For the Waikoloa Beach Marriott renovation, a new
      dining terrace below the lobby offers expanded
      views across a carp pond and coconut grove.
6   The original pool was expanded into a larger
      complex including lap pool, children's sand pool,
      spa, water slide, sunset bar and snack bar.
7   Hilton Waikoloa Village Resort.
8   The Hilton includes an opportunity for guests to
      swim with dolphins under the careful guidance of
      trained attendants.

Large-scale destination resorts throughout the Pacific have long been a specialty for Belt Collins. Nearly 40 years ago, its talents were applied to the now world-famous Mauna Kea Resort, where today the firm still serves as a major design consultant. It was this project, on which Belt Collins worked closely with Laurance Rockefeller and successive owners, that set enduring standards for quality resorts around the world.

Developers and governments in countries all over the Pacific took note of the award-winning design work for Mauna Kea. From that springboard in the late 1960s, Belt Collins was catapulted into the premiere ranks of destination resort design professionals throughout the Pacific and Asia.

In many cases major resort development followed Belt Collins' Visitor Destination Studies, which the firm accomplished for such diverse areas as Thailand, Bali, Hong Kong, the Philippines, Singapore, Ceylon (now Sri Lanka), Malaysia, the Great Barrier Reef and Ayers Rock in Australia, Fiji, Okinawa, China and India.

As is the usual case, the firm provided all of these Asia Pacific destination resorts with one or more of the services from its major skill areas: master planning, land and site planning, civil engineering, landscape architecture, environmental consulting and golf course design.

ASIA/PACIFIC DESTINATION RESORTS

InterContinental Resort, Bali.

1

HAYMAN ISLAND RESORT

Great Barrier Reef, Australia

Client
Ansett Hotels

From the air, Hayman Island in the Great Barrier Reef looks like nothing more than lovely folds of green reaching down to secluded white sand beaches. At first, no structures are visible.

A closer look, however, reveals a luxurious five-star resort, created where for many years only a family-style cluster of vacation cottages existed. The $300 million transformation into a premiere destination resort took place after Belt Collins completed a master plan for the resort and prepared the landscape design for the first phase.

Phase One of the landscaping for the resort cost $7 million. While it included over 650,000 trees, palms and shrubs planted throughout the resort, the idea of landscape simplicity was not lost along the way.

1   Hayman offers a first class resort among one of nature's greatest treasures, the Great Barrier Reef.
Below:
    A pool-within-a-pool is a special feature of the resort.

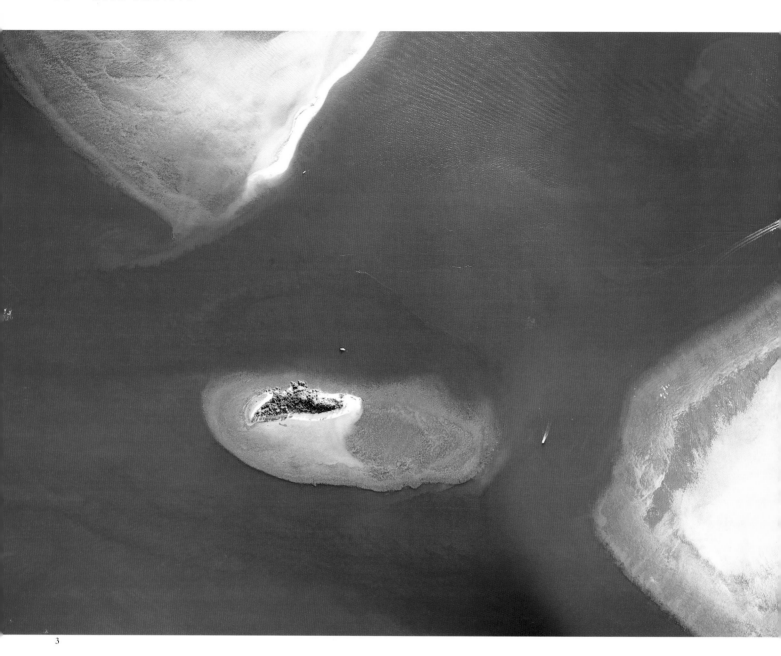

3

4

3 From the air, the resort is barely visible amongst the island's vegetation.
4 Hayman's beauty has attracted dozens of luminaries from around the world.
5 For many years Hayman Island was only a cluster of family cottages.

5

To quote from the resort:

the overall design has been created in such a way as to provide subtle changes as you walk from one area of the resort to another. Some reflect the best of contemporary design and furnishings while others have been carefully created to place the guest in the sumptuous surroundings of a celebrated and bygone era.

Hayman Island presents an irresistible dual attraction: the natural wonders of the huge reef itself and the outstanding flora and fauna of the island combined with a world-class hotel. Muhammad Ali, Kevin Costner, Mariah Carey, Bill Gates, Rupert Murdoch, Tony Blair and the Duke and Duchess of Wellington are a few of the distinguished guests who have been attracted to the Hayman Island Resort.

The Whitsunday Islands, which include Hayman Island, were identified as a destination resort by Belt Collins in its Visitor Destination Study of the Great Barrier Reef, produced for the Australian government.

1

2

LE ROYAL MERIDIEN
BAAN TALING NGAM

Koh Samui, Thailand

Client
Le Meridien Group/First Pacific Land Partners, Ltd.

As it has in so many other cases, Belt Collins sought to enhance the cultural aspects and existing physical conditions in its landscape plan for this residential and destination resort that is sited on an isolated, tree-covered spur of land with beach frontage.

The design concept was sensitive to the site's existing vegetation density and character, incorporating the conservation of six acres of indigenous shrub and woodland, plus numerous rock outcroppings. In addition, 200 trees and a 12-acre wetland were preserved.

The hotel swimming pool landscape includes rooftop lawn terraces, circulation paths and a dramatic sunset promenade. Cultural elements, such as sculpture and art pieces crafted by Thai artists, were used as focal features along the terrace walkways leading to the pool.

Coconut palms emerge from the lower level through structural voids, and large plumeria trees were set around the timber deck. The swimming pool features an infinity edge, Jacuzzi and a pool bar located to maximize views to the sea. A beach club facility comprises a second swimming pool, restaurant and a large deck and garden.

The siting of the villa units followed the concept of a Thai-style village centered around a communal space. Dense bands of vegetation delineate each village cluster, featuring swimming pools with spectacular views to the sea.

3

1   Indigenous style beach pool and restaurant.
2&3   Famous postcard shots from resort's upper pool overlooking
      Andaman Ocean.
4   Low-rise villas nestled in existing coconut grove on a steep slope.

4

1

2

INTERCONTINENTAL RESORT BALI

Jimbaran Beach, Bali, Indonesia

Client
Citra Jimbaran Indah Hotel

The challenge of capturing the uniqueness of Balinese culture throughout a modern beach resort was the aim of the designers when the firm accepted the landscape engagement for the InterContinental Resort Bali.

Water is the main unifying theme of the landscape design. At the entry is a large, formal lotus pool, with swimming pools and water features positioned on the central axis of the main hotel block. Inspiration for the design of the gardens came after Belt Collins designers carried out extensive design research throughout the islands of Bali and Java, in particular the historic water palace pools in Tirtagangga, eastern Bali.

The resort fronts the beautiful and secluded Jimbaran beach. Low-rise hotel structures, designed by architect Hendra Hadiprana, are set within a landscape inspired by both Balinese and Javanese design, that incorporates waterspouts, fire torches, *bales* (Balinese pavilions) and Balinese artwork, carefully placed throughout the gardens.

3

1 Overall view of the resort on the beautiful Jimbaran white sand beach.
2 Tropical landscape integrated into the porte cochere area.
3 Stone waterspout carving.
4 Main swimming pool with thatched *bales* on each side.

4

5

6

5   Feature wall with waterspouts and lily pond.
6   Formal swimming pool with Balinese waterspout sculptures.
7   View from the hotel lobby toward gardens and Kul-Kul tower.
8   Night view of main swimming pool.
9   Presidential suites pool with poolside *bales*.

8

7

9

1 Most visible element is the roof forms since most structures are absorbed by the landscape.
2 The resort was sited around an existing stream.
3 Design and construction utilized local craftsmen and customs.
4 Sunrise along the east coast of Malaysia.
5 The spacious beaches of Tanjong Jara.

TANJONG JARA RESORT

Kuala Terengganu, Malaysia

Client
*Malaysian Government Tourism
Development Council*

A comprehensive tourism plan prepared in 1971, in which Belt Collins played a major part, identified the east coast of Malaysia as an ideal location for a major destination resort. From that study, the resort project was conceived and developed by the Malaysian government. The site chosen for the hotel and a nearby visitor center was a white sand beach and bay that is among the world's few remaining hatcheries for the giant leatherback and green turtles.

With that challenge, the firm worked with the government to develop the environmentally sensitive site as a conservation area and accompanying sea life museum. The landscape plan was specifically designed to incorporate and reflect the indigenous culture and environment of Malaysia's northeast peninsula. A botanical garden and craft bazaar that showcased local arts and crafts were among the facilities Belt Collins incorporated into the project.

Set among this natural landscape are buildings modeled after the indigenous *istanas*, the elegantly crafted wooden palaces of the Malaysian sultans. Belt Collins worked with the architectural firm of Wimberly Allison Tong & Goo to assist local craftspeople in relearning traditional building skills to construct the resort almost exclusively of local hardwood timber.

Malaysian arts and crafts were used throughout with decorative motifs including wood carvings, woven mats, baskets, kites and ceramics. The Tanjong Jara Beach Hotel and Rantau Abang Visitors' Center was awarded the prestigious Aga Khan Award in 1983.

4

5

1

3

2

4

HOTEL NIKKO ROYAL LAKE
Yangon, Myanmar

Client
City Realty Co., Ltd.

Easy circulation from the interior to the exterior is one of the hallmarks of this exceptional hotel, overlooking Yangon's Royal Lake in Myanmar. The building's architects and the landscape architects were especially conscious of the need for openness, a traditional feature of Burmese design. Gallery-like spaces are connected by broad airy verandas and walkways, and the white walls and multi-tiered roofs are softened by lush foliage.

The designers found inspiration in many places. The boundary walls and entry portal were inspired by features at the Mandalay Royal Palace. The swimming pool tile pattern was inspired by traditional Burmese textile designs, and the rectilinear pool was inspired by water tanks found in both Burmese culture and throughout the cultures of South and Southeast Asia.

The hotel landscape is punctuated by multi-tiered pagodas with authentic detailing, crafted by the same carpenter who maintains similar structures at the historic Shwedagon Pagoda, the country's pre-eminent Buddhist shrine.

5

1 Guest room view of reflecting pool, stepped cascade and swimming pool.
2 Pool tile pattern of traditional Burmese textile.
3 Cast bronze figurative sculpture at poolside.
4 Existing majestic raintrees were retained and integrated into the design.
5 Swimming pool in the welcome shade of coconut palms.
6 Reflecting pool with royal lake beyond.

6

8

7

7 Traditional multi-tiered pavilions were constructed by
   local craftsmen.
8 Statuary near the main pool.
9 View of central garden space from inside restaurant.
10 Burmese pots at children's pool.
11 Grand stepped cascade connecting upper and
   reflecting pool and swimming pool.
12 A grid of coconut palms provides a dense canopy over
   the pool area.

9

10

11

12

1

2

1.4 M

3

BANYAN TREE BINTAN

Bintan Island, Indonesia

Client
Tropical Resorts, Ltd.

Barely 30 miles south of Singapore is a boutique resort, which consists of 27 villas perched on a dramatic coastal headland, set amidst rainforest trees. The site has a commanding view of a gently curving bay called Tanjong Said, with the South China Sea beyond.

The Banyan Tree Bintan Resort is only part of the master plan for the 54,360-acre Bintan International Beach Resort, one of the largest created by Belt Collins.

The Banyan Tree is an excellent example of the firm's environmentally sensitive design, where Belt Collins has retained and enhanced the existing natural beauty and drama of the site. The firm worked closely with the resort architects, Architrave Design and Planning, on positioning the hotel and villas, as well as vehicular and pedestrian circulation, to ensure that there was minimal impact to the existing forest trees and large boulder outcrops on the site.

Banyan Tree Bintan is a complete resort with direct access to a white sand beach, two dramatic swimming pools (one of which is set within the mature forested slopes of the resort and a second located adjacent to the beach), and an 18-hole Greg Norman-designed championship golf course. In addition, there are snorkeling, sailing, fishing and numerous other land and beach activities.

The firm also prepared the landscape plan for the Banyan Tree Phuket in Thailand and the Banyan Tree Vabbinfaru in the Maldives, based on environmentally sensitive principles similar to those employed for the Banyan Tree Bintan.

4

1   Native forest plants like this bird's nest fern were used
     as dramatic accents in the landscape.
2   Hillside swimming pool carefully located within the
     existing forest.
3&4 Views from elevated hillside villa.
5   Banyan Tree Bintan's dramatic headland location.

5

6

6 Beachside swimming pool.
7 Elevated hillside villas located amongst mature forest trees.
8 Hotel logo on granite entry feature wall.
9 Hillside swimming pools carefully located within the existing forest.

7

8

9

1 Landscape and ocean view from hotel suite.
2 Swimming pool area with Portuguese-style feature arch linking to the main function lawn.
3 Performance area surrounded by lagoon swimming pool.
4 Goan village character of the resort's villas area.
5 Terraces constructed of local laterite stone.
6 Banquet lawn and feature wall.
7 Mature coconut palms were extensively planted throughout the resort.

TAJ EXOTICA
Goa, India

Client
Taj Group of Hotels

5

6

This resort takes full advantage of the main geographic features of South Goa, its wide, sandy, palm-fringed beaches and crystal clear waters. The 56-acre property is set right on the Arabian Sea, which produces an inviting, balmy climate.

In addition to its attractive physical aspects, Goa benefits from a fascinating blend of Indian and Portuguese influences.

Belt Collins worked side by side with the project architects, Fox Hawaii International, to create the theme of a Goan village, a rich mixture of traditional Indian and Portuguese Colonial styles. The firm carried out an extensive study of Goan vernacular design and incorporated elements and features into many aspects of the resort landscape design.

Set among the exquisitely landscaped lawns, tropical plants and graceful palms are Portuguese gates and feature walls, artwork, balustrades and Azulejos tiled accents.

7

Other Significant Belt Collins Asia Pacific Destination Resorts:

Dusit Laguna, Phuket, Thailand

Denarau Resort, Fiji

Penang Mutiara, Malaysia

Yulara Resort, Australia

Busena Resort, Okinawa, Japan

1

2

3

4

5

1 Dusit Laguna, Phuket, Thailand.
2 Yulara Resort, Ayers Rock, Australia, based on Belt Collins'
   1969 Visitor Destination Study.
3 Busena Resort in Okinawa was developed as a result of a
   recent comprehensive master plan prepared by Belt Collins.
4 Large pool complex at Denarau Resort, Fiji.
5 Floral designs within the pool and water sculpture make
   Mutiara Resort in Penang, Malaysia unique.

One of Belt Collins' proudest achievements is the work the firm has accomplished for the Shangri-La Hotel chain, spanning a 35-year period and 28 properties.

It all started when Robert Kuok, originator of the hotel chain, was searching for a way to make his hotels unique. In 1967 he went to Hawai'i where he was impressed with the landscape design work of Belt Collins. Based on what he saw, he hired the firm to design the gardens for his first hotel—the Shangri-La Singapore.

A good demonstration of Belt Collins' creativity and willingness to try new methods arose when the project landscape architect suggested planting mature trees and palms in the gardens of the Shangri-La Singapore. Two problems became obvious immediately. First, no nursery in Singapore had mature trees available. Advertisements were run asking people to sell their own trees for the project, which many did. The second problem developed when it came time to move the trees. Using techniques developed by Belt Collins in Hawai'i, 'instant trees' were installed. This was when the garden image of Shangri-La was born.

As the hotel chain expanded from urban hotels into resort hotels, Belt Collins continued to provide the design of the landscape and the hardscape, as well as the continuing maintenance programming of their numerous hotel gardens throughout Asia.

The depth of the relationship between Belt Collins and the hotel's owners is best described by **Robert Kuok**, founder of the Shangri-La hotel chain:

Like all successful ventures, it was brilliant teamwork which helped create the Shangri-La Hotel chain. Belt Collins was a vital part of the team.

When I first met the late Walter Collins, I was deeply impressed by his very sincere personality and his great love of nature. Ray Cain came and he succeeded in creating the beautiful gardens of the Shangri-La Hotel in Singapore. More Shangri-La Hotels followed and they all benefited from the landscaping magic woven by the landscape architects of Belt Collins.

The Shangri-La Hotel Group will be forever grateful to Belt Collins for their invaluable contribution.

Whether applied to Shangri-La urban or resort hotels, the overall design philosophy is one of 'bold simplicity'. A small range of garden plant varieties is used in massive sweeps of color and texture, with combinations of color contrasts and structuring of plant groups on varying levels.

The principles of Feng-Shui were subtly applied in the landscape of most Shangri-La hotel properties. Feng-Shui is the Chinese art or practice in which all elements are in harmony with their environment (angles, orientation, wind, direction of water flow and the like).

One of the firm's greatest contributions has been to offer each hotel an appropriate 'sense of place' that reflects its history, culture or other identifiable characteristics that reflect the spirit of the particular region. Within the gardens, this can be found in the use of local building materials, construction techniques, artwork, local indigenous plants and landscape settings appropriate for cultural displays.

SHANGRI-LA HOTELS

Below:
Shangri-La Hotel Surabaya

*Like all successful ventures, it was brilliant
teamwork which helped create the Shangri-La
Hotel chain. Belt Collins was a vital part
of the team.*

Robert Kuok, founder of the Shangri-La hotel chain.

SHANGRI-LA HOTEL
Singapore

When it was built in 1969, this hotel helped to set the landscape standard for not only Shangri-La Hotels, but many others throughout Asia. Before Belt Collins turned this property into a large urban garden, most hotels in the region paid little heed to the landscape as a major component of their hotel package.

Belt Collins also took on the challenge of the garden wing expansion in 1982. In contrast with the narrow high-rise form of the original hotel, for the new low-rise wing, the owners wanted larger, more luxurious rooms, and not simply an annex.

2

Opposite:
  Central waterfall and koi pond serve as focal points from lobby and entry to garden wing.
2 External landscape of garden wing meant to absorb the architecture.
3 Landscaped interior atrium and streams create the mood for garden wing.

3

4

5

6

7

The goal was to fuse the exterior with the interior of the hotel. The result is a vast tropical atrium that soars nine stories within the low-rise new wing. A spectacular two-story waterfall cascades into a rock-lined koi pond below, amid lush tropical foliage.

The lush tropical garden atmosphere was further enhanced through the dense planting on balconies for each guest room. The open corridors give guests dramatic views of the tropical atrium from wherever they are in the hotel.

To demonstrate the sheer scope of the garden motif, over 45,000 plants including 110 varieties of palms, trees, ferns, vines and rows of red bougainvillea were grown in a project nursery before being installed in the 15 acres that made up the firm's work. That work included pathways, water features, pool and terrace layouts, exterior lighting, a botanical park and recreational facilities, including a par-three golf complex.

Over the years the hotel's gardens and pool environment have undergone three major renovations, all designed by Belt Collins, to assure its position as one of the premier hotels in Asia.

4   Freeform pool serves as a focal point for all hotel rooms.
5   Night lighting of landscape environment.
6   Central pool area with Valley Wing beyond.
7   Central pool area with Garden Wing beyond.
8   Water jets enhance the night environment of pool area.

8

9 Central waterfall also serves as a tropical plant display.
10 Vaulted forms of garden wing balconies are a
    Shangri-La architectural trademark designed by
    Wimberly Allison Tong & Goo.
11 Landscaped pool environment as seen from the upper
    walkway.
12 Fountains provide cooling sound and plants provide
    shade necessary within a tropical environment.
13 Landscape serves as a view buffer for poolside guests.

9

10

11

12

13

1

1&2 Importance of sidewalks to define shapes.
  3 Water meanders through grounds.
  4 Golden Sands Resort: first super pool in Asia complete with slides, walking edge, all surrounded by rocks and lush vegetation.

2

SHANGRI-LA'S GOLDEN SANDS RESORT

Penang, Malaysia

3

Prior to this Shangri-La hotel being built in 1985, Asian resort hotels had usually been sited directly adjacent to beaches. The Golden Sands turned out to be different from other resort hotels in the region because Belt Collins, working with architect Robert Fox, AIA, was able to persuade the owners to move the main hotel structure back a considerable distance from the beach line.

The designers saw the opportunity for using the huge area created by the setback for guest activities. In those early days, however, there were no guidelines for using this space, so Belt Collins seized on a unique methodology.

Standing on an upper floor of the unfinished hotel, the Belt Collins landscape architect in charge would call out instructions to workers below who would then mark in chalk on the ground the various design elements and desirable visual composition.

While the essential design elements can be seen repeated around the world, the result of that early work by Belt Collins was a precedent-setting series of free-form pools with islands and waterslides, lawn areas for sunning and resting, curving paths leading from the hotel to the beach, trees and foliage for shade and a multi-purpose court.

4

1

2

3

SHANGRI-LA'S RASA SENTOSA RESORT
Singapore

Belt Collins was first engaged by the government of Singapore to create a master plan and economic feasibility plan for the 667-acre Sentosa Island in 1969. With its close proximity to downtown Singapore, the master plan called for a major resort/recreation complex including resorts, commercial facilities, hotels, picnic grounds, sports fields and beaches. This was quite a change from what was originally a fishing village and, until 1967, a British military fortress.

As the prime consultant of a team of specialists in the 1980s, the firm was responsible for the planning, coastal engineering and landscape architecture of a major beach reclamation and improvement project for nearly one mile of beachfront on the island.

Once that monumental work was done, the Shangri-La hotel chain decided to work with the firm to site its planned resort directly adjacent to the curved lagoon created by Belt Collins.

Today, the Shangri-La Rasa Sentosa sits amidst a landscape environment that includes a free-form lagoon pool, waterslides, water features and gardens on an island for which Belt Collins prepared the master plan and designed the beach reclamation.

4

1&5 Only minutes from downtown Singapore, Rasa Sentosa is a comprehensive resort destination facing a man-made beach.
2 Looking south with beach and lagoon under construction.
3 A guest's view of the pool and recreation area.
4 Beach and lagoon created by Belt Collins engineers and landscape architects.

5

1

2

1&2 Shade pavilion with Malay roof at end of pool.
   3 The pool features an overflow edge and adjacent large boulders set within existing shoreline trees.
   4 Swimming pool and children's poolside tree slide.

3

SHANGRI-LA'S
RASA SAYANG RESORT
Penang, Malaysia

The first Shangri-La beach resort was the Rasa Sayang in Penang, Malaysia. Set amid 15 acres of lush gardens, the hotel has long been a favorite of vacationers throughout the world, because it offers the tranquility of a tropical paradise along with luxurious accommodation.

Among the outstanding features of the hotel's landscape are the swimming pools, which were designed in two increments by Belt Collins. One of the pools is free-form with existing large raintrees incorporated into the design. Using those trees, the firm created a unique three-story tree house with a special children's slide into the pools.

The pool design incorporated an infinity edge plus a sloping beach entry. Rockwork boulders form another side of the pool, creating continuity with the nearby white sand beach and shoreline boulders.

In keeping with the firm's desire to create a 'sense of place' for the Shangri-La Rasa Sayang, traditional Malay-style thatched huts are dotted along the beach to provide shade and gathering spots for hotel guests.

5

6

8

7

5 Poolside tree slide built around existing mature raintree.
6 View toward the renovated pool.
7 Organic salt pool with lush surrounding landscape.
8 Swimming pool and children's poolside tree slide.
9 The pool features an overflow edge and adjacent large
   boulders set within existing shoreline trees.

9

1

SHANGRI-LA HOTEL SURABAYA

Surabaya, Indonesia

This five-star hotel is a typical example of the way Belt Collins creates a 'sense of identity' by incorporating elements of the local culture into the overall landscape design.

The challenge for Belt Collins in this city hotel was to create an urban oasis far removed from the hustle and bustle of Indonesia's second largest city. Inspired by the magical forms, materials and colors of East Java, the firm incorporated stylized rice terraces, waterfalls and swimming lagoons, as well as local plant species, into their design for the hotel.

A wide range of Javanese stone types, building materials, and traditional construction techniques were used throughout the project. Particular attention was given to the design of the numerous hand-carved stone feature panels (some 15 meters long), sculpture pots and water spouts, which are strategically positioned throughout the hotel gardens.

1 Guest wing view of swimming pool and waterfall.
2 Carved stone (batu paras) feature wall.
3 Water spouts add to design of unique feature wall.

2

3

Other Significant Belt Collins Shangri-La Hotel Projects:

Shangri-La's Mactan Island Resort, Cebu, Philippines

Shangri-La Hotel, Beijing, China

Island Shangri-La, Hong Kong

Shangri-La's Fijian Resort, Fiji

Edsa Shangri-La, Manila, Philippines

Shangri-La Hotel, Bangkok, Thailand

1

2

1 Island Shangri-La with peaceful garden and pool set against dramatic high-rise architecture of Hong Kong's central business district.
2 Shangri-La Hotel, Beijing with garden displays for four seasons.
3 Shangri-La's Mactan Island Resort in Cebu, Philippines features a massive man-made beach carved from coral cliffs.

3

5

4   Pool edge at Shangri-La's Fijian Resort.
5   At the Edsa Shangri-La in Manila crafted planters filled with
    rich tropical plants define window outlook.
6   Guest view of pool, palm tree-lined sundeck, poolside bar
    and riverside at Shangri-La Hotel, Bangkok.

6

In any society, in any place on earth, people seek recreation as a way of enhancing their lives. Belt Collins, providing master planning, landscape architecture, engineering design and environmental consulting, has accomplished that enhancement around the world via golf courses, tennis complexes, parks, racetracks, football and soccer practice fields, aquatic centers and water parks, track and field venues including Olympic and Asian Games facilities, and many more.

When the firm creates a master plan for a resort or a community, a golf course can be the single largest land use within it, creating the major open space, view corridor and visual amenity. Thus, careful consideration must be given to such elements as landscape transitions from the course to roadways and major entry, to residential areas and to the hotel itself.

In all its diverse recreational endeavors, Belt Collins is mindful of the need to balance the fun aspects of a project with the practical, in terms of maintenance and sustainability. Where appropriate, the firm always attempts to make extensive use of available native plant material and local cultural elements.

As former Philippines First Lady **Amelita M. Ramos** said of the firm,

In their wonderfully created landscapes, Belt Collins shows us a world of man and nature that is not in contradiction with each other. Its many projects around the world, including those in the Philippines, are inspired creations that highlight and build on the beauty and strength of nature.

RECREATIONAL DEVELOPMENTS

Singapore Turf Club.

1   Plaza paving design based on Aboriginal motifs.
2   One of three pools designed for dual use, during the Olympics and afterwards.
3   Entry pylon that announces venue and provides clear direction.
4&5 Overhead of stadium and aquatic center with Belt Collins designed plazas in foreground.

1

2

SYDNEY INTERNATIONAL ATHLETIC AND AQUATIC CENTRES

Homebush, New South Wales, Australia

Client
Civil and Civic

When a potential host country is in the running to compete for an Olympic venue, the immediate need is for developable sites for the various sporting activities. That was the case in Sydney, where the city and national governments turned to many underutilized sites in their bid to accommodate various new athletic venues.

Because of their experience in successfully transforming degraded sites all around the Pacific, the landscape architects at Belt Collins were called in to do just that in Sydney.

Belt Collins, working with client Civil and Civic, the Olympic Committee and architects Philip Cox, Richardson, Taylor & Partners and Peddle Thorpe, master planned and designed the pre-Olympic venues that were instrumental in Sydney's winning bid.

Once Sydney was chosen, the firm took a derelict site and, through unification of the architecture and landscape, were able to set new design standards for sporting facilities. Always aware of the need to integrate local styles, the designers created an Aquatic Centre Garden and Athletic Centre Concourse that translated a strong Australian identity through the use of plant materials, patterns and shapes.

Through conservation and reuse of resources throughout the project, the firm was able to achieve maximum value for the public monies used. As a result of the design and conservation efforts, Sydney Olympic International Athletic and Aquatic Centres received an International Olympic Committee Award.

3

4

5

1

2

3

1 Still restless Pinatubo in the background with new golf course.
2 Very little plant life after area was covered with ash.
3 Mini golf and putting green are part of the golf complex.
4 Restored fairway of Mimosa Golf Course showing preserved rain trees.
5 Clark Air Base in the Philippines devastated by Mt. Pinatubo volcanic eruption.
6 Air base after transformation.

4

MIMOSA GOLF
& COUNTRY CLUB
Clarkfield, Philippines

Client
Mondragon International Philippines, Inc.

When a simmering volcano finally erupted in the Pinatubo area of the Philippines in 1991, three to ten feet of ash were hurled onto the existing military golf course at Clark Air Base, a sprawling U.S. military facility. The ash destroyed the old course, yet it left many of the majestic raintrees, which subsequently were carefully revived and integrated into the new landscape design for the golf course created by Belt Collins.

Today there is a spectacular clubhouse, golf academy, putting course and a remodeled 27-hole course, for which Belt Collins provided the master planning, golf course architecture and landscape design, in conjunction with its former sister company Nelson & Haworth. The golf course was completed in a record-setting 11 months, due to the Philippine government's fast-track legislation and the efforts of the designers and builders.

If it weren't for the ingenuity of the Belt Collins professionals, others might still be struggling with the problems of what to do with the massive amounts of volcanic ash, or lahar, left behind by the volcano. What they discovered was that the lahar was an excellent source of potash, which when mixed with the existing soil and other fertilizers, provided great growing conditions.

This golf course is another example of transforming a devastated site into a beautiful landscape environment through design innovation.

5

6

Belt Collins shows us a world of man and nature that is not in contradiction…its many projects around the world are inspired creations that highlight and build on the beauty and strength of nature.

Amelita M. Ramos, former Philippines First Lady

FRANCIS H. I'I BROWN GOLF COURSES

Mauna Lani Resort, Kohala, Hawai'i, USA

Client
Mauna Lani Resort

2

Opposite:
  The shoreline becomes an important part of Mauna Lani's
  signature hole.
2&3   Unique lava formations were incorporated into golf course design.

3

Many superlatives have been showered on this golf course, such as 'this golf course transcends art'.

For more than a decade the course served as the venue for the annual Senior Skins Golf Tournament. This competition saw such greats of the PGA Seniors as Arnold Palmer, Jack Nicklaus, Lee Trevino, Gary Player, Raymond Floyd and Hale Irwin.

Because of Belt Collins' experience and success with the Mauna Kea Resort on the Kohala Coast, the firm was selected to master plan the entire 3,200-acre Mauna Lani Resort. The property is located on a 16th century lava flow, so not only were the planners and designers faced with the huge mass of lava, but also the preservation of 15 acres of ancient spring-fed Hawaiian fishponds, as well as archeological sites and the King's Trail, a traditional pathway.

For the golf course, Belt Collins chose to showcase the lava as the course's main feature. The layout is a study in simplicity and contrasts: brilliant green spaces sculpted among the stark black and brown landmass. One reviewer described the juxtaposition as 'a Zen-like garden blooming in the midst of a stark, forbidding wasteland'.

The owners wanted a course with continual challenges, so golfers would come away with one special thing to remember about each hole. Ask any Mauna Lani course player, and they will tell you how well that was done.

While the original 18-hole course was opened in 1981, ten years later the course was integrated into nine new holes added to the front nine to create the South Course, and nine new holes added to the back nine to make up the North Course. Both the Francis H. I'i Brown North and South are championship courses. Belt Collins also accomplished this work.

The golf course architects were Belt Collins and their successor firm Nelson & Wright, Golf Course Architects.

4

5

4   View of Mauna Lani Golf Course looking toward the mountains.
5   The ocean and black lava were integrated into the golf course
    as important design elements.
6&10   Contrast of green grass with black lava.
7–9   Golfers are constantly challenged by natural hazards.

6

7

Nelson and Haworth's best work was accomplished with Belt Collins' team of planners, landscape architects and engineers. This collaboration resulted in numerous golf course projects over two decades in Europe, Asia, Australia, the mainland U.S. and many Pacific islands.

Robin Nelson, Golf Course Architect

8

9

10

1 Entry with elevated rapid transit tracks beyond.
2 Arrival plaza with monumental numerical sculptures.
3 VIP entry roundabout.

1

SINGAPORE TURF CLUB

Singapore

Client
Singapore Turf Club

For Belt Collins' landscape professionals, this project was based on nostalgia. They were asked by the owners to create a mature landscape like that at the old Bukit Timah Racecourse, which was representative of the Singapore of long ago—a lush landscape with beautiful raintrees, very large scale and almost park-like.

During the three years of planning and design work for the new racecourse and surrounding facilities, the owners and the firm's designers considered transplanting the distinctive grove of junipers from the old to the new site, as one means of recreating what went before. The idea seemed too risky, however, and so new large-scale specimens were planted instead.

A balance was developed by the designers through the use of trees, shrubs and design elements from the old racecourse, combined with the bold use of red, green and gold foliage hedges in the shape of supergraphic stars, to recall the distinctive graphic patterns found on racing silks, for the new racecourse.

The finished project has been described as having the ambience of a classical Singaporean landscape–soothing, beautiful and timeless.

2

3

1 Many existing trees were preserved in place and others moved
  to be included in the golf courses.
Below:
  Shoreline aerial looking south in early stages of development.
3 Wailea golf with fairway residential development.
4 Aerial of entire 1,450-acre Wailea Resort complex that includes
  five white sand beaches, five world-class hotels, and three
  championship golf courses, a new shopping center and
  numerous residences.

1

WAILEA RESORT
Wailea, Hawai'i, USA

Client
Wailea Development Company

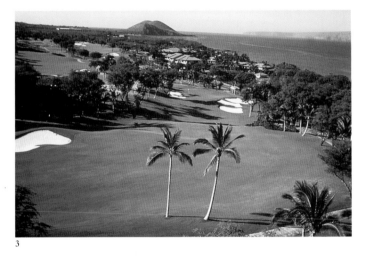

3

When the first master plan was prepared for the Wailea Resort, the designers began with a two-mile long and one-mile wide property of mostly arid, kiawe mesquite thicket along the south shore of Maui. Hot and dry, the area had brackish water with a high chloride content.

Existing trees were fully mature monkeypods, kiawe and native wili wili with three-foot diameter trunks. The idea was to preserve as many of these trees as possible, which required relocating many of them from existing to proposed fairways.

It has been said that the genius of Belt Collins' residential land planning is the great attention given to creating, directing and framing memorable views. For the Blue Course, designed in the 1970s by Arthur Jack Snyder, the firm set a design goal to enhance the relationship of homes and condominiums to the golf courses.

In the mid-'90s, working with Robert Trent Jones, Jr. on the Gold and Emerald Courses, the firm created bands of native plant material laid out to complement the original lava flows down Haleakala. Very old cattle walls were worked into the design, and, taking that element further, the firm created extensive meandering lava walls as a playful but functional interpretation of the originals.

Today the resort includes handsome single-family residences, stately hotels and three world-class golf courses. A tree canopy is the dominant feature of the overall development. The Senior Skins Tourney, played for years at the Mauna Lani Resort, has moved to the Wailea Gold Course in the 21st century.

4

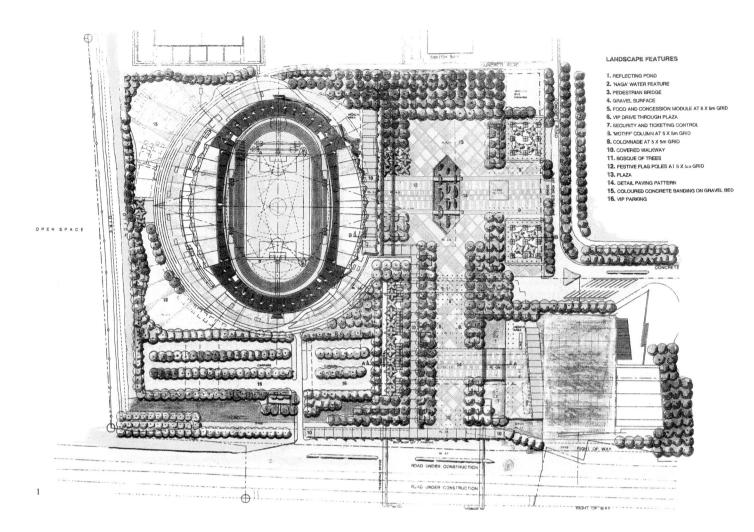

OPEN SPACE

LANDSCAPE FEATURES

1. REFLECTING POND
2. 'NAGA' WATER FEATURE
3. PEDESTRIAN BRIDGE
4. GRAVEL SURFACE
5. FOOD AND CONCESSION MODULE AT 6 X 6m GRID
6. VIP DRIVE THROUGH PLAZA
7. SECURITY AND TICKETING CONTROL
8. 'MOTIFF' COLUMN AT 5 X 5m GRID
9. COLONNADE AT 5 X 5m GRID
10. COVERED WALKWAY
11. BOSQUE OF TREES
12. FESTIVE FLAG POLES AT 5 X 5m GRID
13. PLAZA
14. DETAIL PAVING PATTERN
15. COLOURED CONCRETE BANDING ON GRAVEL BED
16. VIP PARKING

1

2

ASIAN GAMES
RANGSIT SPORTS COMPLEX
Rangsit, Pathumthani, Thailand

Client
Thammasat University

Among the functional planning and landscape aspects of this large project was the desire to create a strong and memorable image and an exciting festive atmosphere for the games. Large volumes of visitors and participants had to be able to proceed to and from the venues safely and conveniently. Considered were the future use of the facilities in the post-Games mode as well as environmental factors, historical context and the way public spaces are used and enjoyed in Thailand.

The landscape design concept used the organizational device of a traditional Thai pedestrian spine or main street, oriented on a north-south axis. Sequential design elements or functional nodes were strategically located along the main street with strong Thai, yet internationally recognized, characteristics.

At the front of the plaza, the featured design highlights the large *naga* sculptures complementing each other in a large reflecting pond. In Thailand, *nagas* symbolize the guardians of fair play and serve as a strong icon for this international tournament. Colonnades, flagpoles and special Thai patterns complete the cultural context of the design.

3

1   Landscape Master Plan
2   Thai *naga* symbolize goodwill and fairness.
3   View of urban landscape designed for games.
4   Formal landscape features reinforce axial planning.

4

1

2

WAIPIO SOCCER COMPLEX

Waipahu, Hawai'i, USA

Client
City and County of Honolulu

Belt Collins was faced with several environmental challenges right from the beginning of this project to build 19 regulation-size soccer fields on 140 acres of former sugar cane land owned by the U.S. Navy.

One of the greatest challenges was to develop a master plan, program requirements, engineering plans, preparation of environmental documents and a lease execution document, in less than 12 months.

Among the services provided by the firm were soils boring and soils sampling for chemical and physical characteristics and preparation of environmental baseline and health risk assessment documents to satisfy the Navy's leasing requirements.

Needless to say, Belt Collins was up to the monumental task of completing this documentation for three levels of government and of starting construction–all within the prescribed 12-month period.

The firm provided master planning, civil engineering, environmental consulting and landscape architecture for the entire project.

3

1&2 Soccer heaven for players of all ages.
  3 Start of construction for 19 regulation-size soccer fields where
     Belt Collins provided civil engineering, environmental consulting
     and landscape architecture on 140 acres of former sugar land.
4&5 Teams from around the world compete.

4   5

Other Significant Belt Collins Recreation Projects:

Star City Casino, Sydney, Australia

Pearl Harbor Historic Trail, Oahu, Hawai'i, USA

Lana'i Pines Sporting Clays, Lana'i, Hawai'i, USA

Rainbow Run, Redmond, Washington, USA

University of Hawai'i Athletic Practice Fields, Honolulu, Hawai'i, USA

Pineapple Garden Maze at Dole Plantation, Wahiawa, Hawai'i, USA

Splash Island Leisure Park, Manila, Philippines

Kapalua Golf Course, Kapalua, Hawai'i, USA

1

2

1   Star City Casino, Sydney, Australia.
2   Pearl Harbor Historic Trail, Hawai'i.
3   Lana'i Pines Sporting Clays, Lana'i, Hawai'i.
4   Rainbow Run, Redmond, Washington.

3

4

5

6

7

8

5   University of Hawai'i athletic practice fields.
6   Golf Villas sited to overlook Arnold Palmer-designed
       Kapalua Bay Course.
7   Aerial view of Kapalua Resort, Hawai'i.
8   Splash Island Leisure Park in Manila, Philippines.
9&10 Hawai'i's Pineapple Garden Maze at Dole Plantation
       was named in the 2001 Guinness Book of Records as
       the largest in the world.

9

10

When successful, land developments and building projects are enhanced in opportunity and value by their transformation. For many years Belt Collins has been involved with these transformations throughout the world, whether of structures or plots of land.

The firm's practice is to become involved with owners from the beginning, as they lay out their vision for the transformation of a piece of property. For owners who want a coordinated effort, that early work leads to Belt Collins assembling a team that includes creative professionals from all its major disciplines—master planning, landscape architecture, civil engineering, environmental consulting and, if called for, golf course design.

Perhaps Belt Collins' many skills in the area of transforming properties is best described by a longtime client **Richard C. Helfer**, Chairman and CEO, Raffles International Ltd., based in Singapore:

Belt Collins in their collaboration with us on our Raffles Hotel, Raffles Hotel Le Royal and Raffles Grand Hotel d'Angkor have refined the tropical garden into an art form through their appreciation of the way landscape can transform the site environment, which lifts and inspires the human spirit. This has been done while showcasing the historical buildings in a proper manner consistent throughout all three of our Raffles properties.

There are numerous examples throughout the Pacific basin of the transformations in which Belt Collins played an integral part. These include a destination resort built on an old tin mine, a canoe-racing sports area carved out of a backwater lagoon, and the restoration of several historic hotels, including a monumental post office that has been turned into a sophisticated urban hotel.

Belt Collins in their collaboration with us ...have refined the tropical garden into an art form... which lifts and inspires the human spirit.

Richard C. Helfer, Chairman and CEO, Raffles International Ltd.

Opposite:
Raffles Grand Hotel d'Angkor

TRANSFORMATIONS

1

2

3

5

4

RAFFLES HOTEL
Singapore

Client
Raffles International Ltd.

6

7

1   Front façade and entry area.
2   Planting of mature Livistona Rotundifolia palm at Palm Court.
3,4&6   Views of Palm Court.
5   View of swimming pool.
7   Night view of palm garden with historic fountain.

Somerset Maugham, a frequent guest, called Raffles, 'the hotel that stands for all the fables of the Exotic East'. With loving care, Raffles Hotel, thought by many to be synonymous with the image of Singapore, has been provided an exceptional restoration. The return of the hotel to its former glory came from a cooperative effort between the Singapore government, a private developer and Raffles International Ltd.

Equal attention was given to the restoration of the gardens, because throughout the long and colorful history of the hotel (it was built in 1887), the gardens have always played a large part in creating the property's overall ambience. With acquisition of land over the years, the hotel gardens now cover nearly one quarter of the property and consist of six enclosed courtyards of varying themes and character: the original Palm Court plus the newer Fern Court, the Palm Garden, Raffles Courtyard, Raffles Square and The Lawn.

After extensive research into the hotel's original landscape planting, materials and features, the firm's design resolutely supported the careful protection, and in some cases transplanting, of the existing mature traveller's palms, Livistona palms and frangipani trees, many of which were over 90 years old. The design for the hotel gardens included over 50,000 plants and 73 species of trees, palms and ferns—all overseen by the hotel's horticulturist.

During the restoration process, Richard Helfer, the CEO of Raffles, found an antique fountain that had been left to rust in a field. He rescued it and through research determined that the fountain was from Telok Ayer Market Place in Singapore, placed there in the early 1800s. Mr. Helfer and Belt Collins worked to renovate the fountain, which now has pride of place in the hotel's Palm Court.

Belt Collins has become the acknowledged expert in the specialized area of historic hotel landscape design. The firm has worked on the restoration and redevelopment of many of Asia's most celebrated historic hotels, such as the Eastern & Oriental Hotel, Penang; The Taj Mahal Hotel, Mumbai; Grand Hotel d'Angkor and the Hotel Le Royal, Cambodia; as well as the Royal Hawaiian Hotel, Hawai'i.

8

9

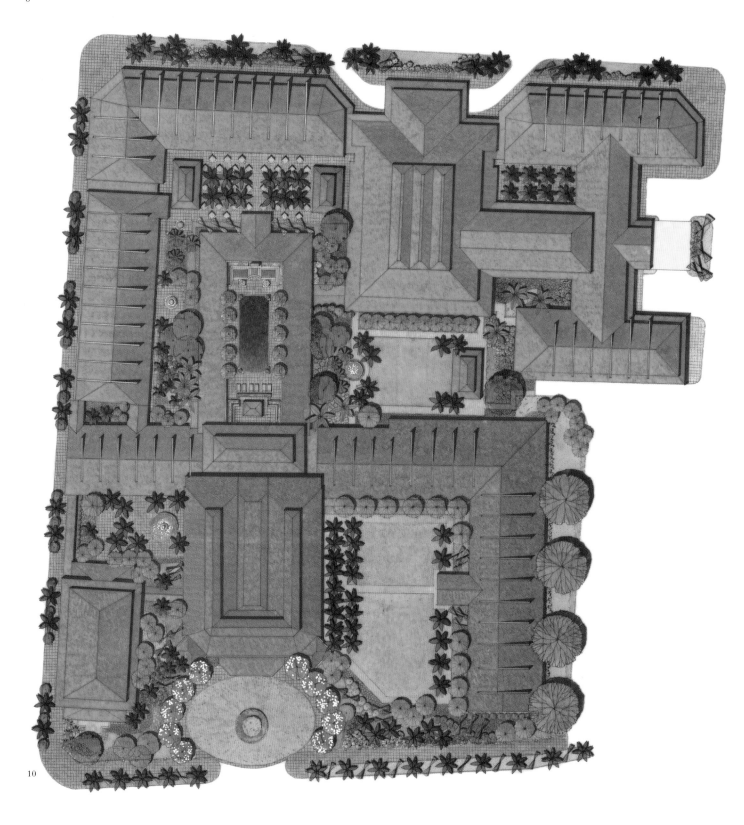

10

11

12

8   Garden view from open guest room corridor.
9   Night view of the hotel.
10   Landscape Master Plan.
11   Livistona Rotundifolia palms at Palm Court.
12   Detail of softscape and hardscape landscape patterns.
13&14   Historic architecture set amidst lush tropical foliage.

13

14

1

2

3

THE FULLERTON HOTEL

Singapore

Client
Sino Land Company Ltd.

1 View of Fullerton before transformation.
2 Boat quay waterfront promenade and alfresco dining area.
3 View of the hotel's location next to historic Singapore River.
4 Monumental granite water-feature urns carved in China.

Built in 1932, the structure was described by the *Straits Times* as follows:

The Post Office Building, with its walls towering 120 feet from the ground, its fluted Doric colonnades on their heavy base, its lofty portico over the main entrance and the 400-foot frontage along the waterfront, adds immeasurably to the dignity and solidity of Central Singapore.

It took three years to bring about the adaptive reuse of the rundown old post office, but the dignity and solidity referred to above have been well preserved. At the same time, the structure has been transformed into a luxury hotel with 400 sleekly modern rooms, world-class dining and meeting facilities.

Working with the architectural firm Architects 61 from Singapore, Belt Collins developed a landscape plan that took advantage of many of the old building's best features. A central atrium was turned into a stunning courtyard featuring bamboo in planters, to carry out the hotel's New Asia theme. A swimming pool was designed atop an adjacent annex building, to complete the hotel's amenities.

4

5   View of infinity-edge swimming pool overlooking
    Singapore River.
6   Colonnade features pots and palms.
7   View of the hotel's location next to historic
    Singapore River.
8   East façade of the Fullerton Hotel.
9   East Garden lily pool, fountain wall and trellis.
10 Night view of East Garden reflective pool.

5

6

7

8

9

10

1

1 Dramatically themed 'Elephant Wall' at night.
2 Khmer sculpture integrating water-theme park.
3 Drawing of proposed Laguna Phuket
4 Aerial view of abandoned tin mine before development.
5 Aerial photo of the resort after transformation.
6 Landscape of the 'Forgotten City'.

2

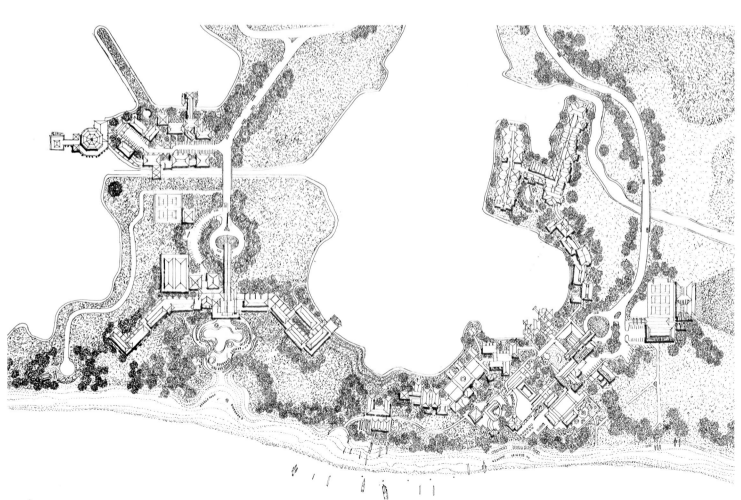

3

LAGUNA PHUKET RESORT
Phuket, Thailand

For years an old tin mine in a prime location languished as barren earth and ponds. The whole area was of little use since it had been abandoned for many years.

Realizing that the area had potential because of its beautiful white sand beaches, Belt Collins was engaged to prepare a master plan.

The reclamation of the old mine into a first class resort remains one of the greatest transformations in the world. Now guests play on the beach, motor and sail around sparkling lagoons and enjoy the amenities of several world class hotels on the property.

4

5

6

Laguna Beach Resort

Client
Laguna Resorts & Hotels

The overall landscape theme the firm chose for the **Laguna Beach Resort** is based on the concept of a stylized Khmer ruined city. For inspiration, the design team studied the original temples at Angkor.

The theme starts from the entrance gate and is carried through to the main swimming pool area. It was accomplished by using extensive rock walls and sculpture, which were hand-carved by a team of local Thai craftsmen.

Besides the beach, the resort offers other sources of water activity in the shape of a tropical lagoon and a self-contained four-acre water park. Various types of pools within the water park were designed to delight guests. Belt Collins created a scuba-diving pool with an underwater carved stonewall. There is also a fun pool with a water slide hiding behind an 'Elephant Wall' with stone warriors. A separate sport pool is set aside for water games and a jacuzzi.

1

2

3

1 Thai architecture doubled in reflecting pool.
2 Derelict tin mine turned into interior recreational
   lagoon.
3 Atmosphere created in different pool niches.
4 Sport and game pool for active guests.
5 Coconut grove enhances the beach atmosphere.

5

4

6

7

8

6 Visual axis to floating pool bar.
7 Swim-up pool bar at dusk.
8 Series of water courts.
9 Main pool with hardscape feature and large
   waterslide hidden behind feature wall.

9

Sheraton Grande Laguna Phuket

Client
Laguna Resorts & Hotels

For the **Sheraton Grande Laguna Phuket**, the landscape design developed by the firm emphasizes traditional Thai cultural elements, which are formal yet simple in design. There are several key elements in the design: the Courtyard, the Promenade, the River and a man-made beach. In traditional Thai town planning, these elements combine the symbolic forces of nature and culture inherent in the existing landscape.

Central to the concept is the Courtyard and the Promenade, which together form a traditional link to the buildings and the 'river'.

The design also features a swimming pool in the form of a meandering river. It wraps around the buildings and carves its way from a symbolic mountain, through a dense garden area, terminating in an artificial-beach swimming pool. Intersecting all four elements is a strong visual axis evident as guests explore the property.

1

3

2

1 Pool along waterfront units.
2 Artificial sand beach brings feel of ocean to interior development.
3 Old tin mine converted to wetlands, lagoons for recreation and connecting canals for intra-resort water transport.

1

2

3

RAFFLES HOTELS

Cambodia

Client
Raffles International Ltd.

Raffles Grand Hotel d'Angkor
Siem Reap, Cambodia

Two of Asia's great historic hotels, Hotel Le Royal and Grand Hotel d'Angkor, have been restored to their former glory by the renowned Raffles International hotel group of Singapore.

Situated on nearly eight acres, the **Grand Hotel d'Angkor** is located on the central axis with the ancient Angkor Wat temple in northwest Cambodia. For many years intrepid travelers have been making their way to the ancient temples, and the hotel was originally built to serve their needs.

For the renovation, the firm made use of the Raffles signature landscape scheme of travellers' palms and frangipani trees. To these were added mature sugar palms, which are indigenous to the area. An exceptionally large swimming pool, inspired by the ancient bathing pools of the Khmer Kings of Angkor, was installed in the grounds.

To underscore the Cambodian character of the hotel's gardens, Belt Collins worked with skilled local craftsmen and local construction materials.

What sets this restored hotel apart from others are the 15-acre public gardens that create an imposing frontage for the property across the way. The Gardens contain four sections, all restored by the client with a design provided by Belt Collins.

4

1 View of children's pool and pool bar pavilion.
2 Pool bar pavilion.
3 Temple garden.
4 View of the hotel from the formal garden.
5 Overall view of pool and surrounding gardens.
6 View of Apsara Terrace stage and function lawn
   set amidst grove of sugar palms.

5

6

Raffles Hotel Le Royal
Phnom Penh, Cambodia

Hotel Le Royal, originally opened in 1931, is of an art-deco architectural design with French Colonial and Khmer influences. During its heyday, Le Royal played host to such luminaries as Somerset Maugham, Jacqueline Kennedy and Charles de Gaulle.

When Raffles International decided to restore the hotel, which reopened in 1997, the company set as its first goal the preservation of the unique French Colonial/Art Deco character of the historic hotel, updated for a modern world-class hostelry.

Belt Collins was responsible for restoration of the extensive gardens that, at six acres, are an important part of the property's overall design. Within the 210-room hotel's central landscaped courtyard are two formal swimming pools, lush planting and custom-made site furnishings. Three majestic raintrees and numerous mature frangipani trees were carefully preserved during renovation of the hotel. More than 25 additional mature frangipani trees were transplanted to the site, together with numerous tropical trees, palms, shrubs and groundcover which were purchased both locally and imported from Vietnam and Thailand.

1 Transplanting of mature frangipani tree.
2 Alfresco dining at café Monivong.
3 View of hotel before transformation.
4 Hotel entry after transformation.
5 Main swimming pool and existing raintree.
6 View of central courtyard garden during renovation.
7 Courtyard garden after renovation.

5

4

6

7

1

2

3

KE'EHI LAGOON CANOE COMPLEX

Honolulu, Hawai'i, USA

Client
State of Hawai'i, Department of Transportation, Harbors Division

In the past several years in Hawai'i, traditional outrigger canoe paddling has seen a resurgence, with annually over one hundred events statewide involving thousands of competitors. Demand for a dedicated course grew, but suitable sites were few.

In recognition of participant demand, the State of Hawai'i engaged Belt Collins to develop a world-class outrigger canoe racecourse and competition center. The site chosen turned out to be a backwater lagoon that was an abandoned dump. The transformation of this site into a popular beach park required deft engineering and innovative landscape design, given the less than ideal site conditions, the unique requirements of the sport and the need to preserve existing park space.

Three important conditions needed to be met: (1) because outrigger canoe racing is a spectator sport, the landscape plan called for grass covered viewing mounds—rather than bleachers—strung along the shore of the park's flat terrain; (2) to make the course fair for all paddlers, it was important to achieve a maximum racecourse width and uniform water depth, which was accomplished through dredging; and (3) an important element was the creation of a beach where canoes could be pulled up for launching and changing crews. This was accomplished using a crushed aggregate as beach nourishment material. Shade trees, restrooms and parking areas completed the plan.

4

1 Aerial view looking west with man-made beach in the foreground.
2&3 Beach and spectator berm under construction.
4 Man-made beach fronts a larger urban park.
5 Ke'ehi Lagoon was transformed from a derelict landfill to a popular competitive canoe-racing complex.

5

1 Belt Collins landscape architect Ray Cain conducted initial site
  survey 28 years before any buildings went up.
2 During the last 20 years, the area has evolved into a premiere
  residential community.
3 All architecture and landscape adhere to strict design standards.
4 Landscape designed to complement the architecture.
5 A variety of water features are displayed throughout the complex.

3

1

2

DISCOVERY BAY

Hong Kong

Client
HKR International Limited

In the early 1970s, Belt Collins provided planning, engineering and landscape architectural services to Hong Kong entrepreneur Eddie Wong for his proposed major urban development on 1,500 acres of Lantau Island in Hong Kong Bay. At the time, Lantau Island was completely undeveloped.

Following the original Belt Collins plan, today Discovery Bay is a massive residential and leisure community developed on Lantau Island's varying terrain. In addition to Discovery Bay, the new Hong Kong International Airport is also located on Lantau. This is the same island where the firm is working on the large Hong Kong Disney project.

Reflecting unique living accommodations, Discovery Bay offers garden houses in a golf course area, vacation apartments in high-rise condominium towers and future hotel rooms. Facilities include a 450-berth marina, swimming pools, playing courts, commercial and community buildings, and a ferry system linking the island with urban Hong Kong and Kowloon. The landscape features a Mediterranean theme including fountains, water features and colorful planting patterns.

4

5

Other Significant Belt Collins Transformation Projects:

Keppel Marina, Singapore

Dole Playground, Honolulu, Hawai'i, USA

Sungei Besi, Malaysia

Palace of the Golden Horses, Kuala Lumpur, Malaysia

Triboa Bay Villas and Clubhouse, Subic Bay, Philippines

Fontana Resort, Clark Field, Philippines

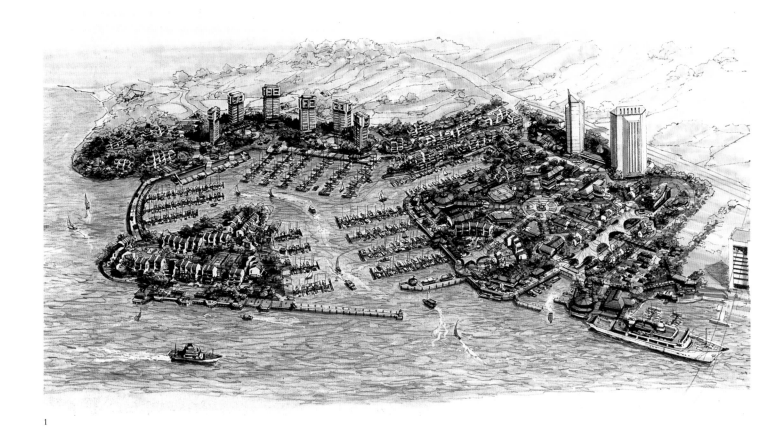

1

1 Perspective of Keppel Marina currently evolving from
   an old shipyard.
2 Dole Playground in Honolulu, Hawai'i was built on an
   old stone quarry.
3 Derelict site, which was the world's oldest tin mine,
   before development of the master plan for Sungei
   Besi with Architects Hawaii.
4 The 13-acre Palace of the Golden Horses includes a
   lake designed in conjunction with architects
   Wimberly Allison Tong & Goo.
5 Local flora and fauna carried out Malaysian influence
   at the Palace of the Golden Horses.

2

3

4

5

6

6   Once an ammunition storage yard, this shoreline at Subic
    Naval Base in the Philippines was transformed into luxury
    villas to accommodate the prestigious APEC meeting in
    1996.
7   The guard house welcomed heads of state from around
    the world.
8   Night view of the Fontana water park in the Philippines.

7

8

Many Asian and Pacific Rim cities are among the world's most interesting. Some of these cities are ancient with wonderful histories; others are newer, yet fascinating in their own right. As in cities anywhere, however, calming spaces—spaces for respite in today's very hectic world—are becoming more and more a requirement of those living and working in urban areas.

Builders, developers and governments have responded to this need in various ways. In many cases urban spaces that could have been just more clutter and noise have been turned into areas of beauty and calm. Belt Collins has transformed a wide variety of projects—such as urban hotels, office buildings, condominiums, sports activities, airports and even shopping areas—by creating pockets of calm in busy cityscapes.

The firm has created these urban spaces with an eye toward sensitivity to local culture and plant life. In one example, Belt Collins planned and executed the moving of a huge historic ficus tree down a river to a new location at a mid-city high rise.

Stuart Hornery, Chairman and CEO of Lend Lease from 1978 to 2000, said of the firm,

I have long been an admirer of the work of Belt Collins. In the early 1980s Lend Lease/Civil and Civic brought Belt Collins to Australia to work with our design teams. Our early association with Jim Bell and Tom Papandrew blossomed into a long-term relationship with their firm. During the ensuing twenty years, Belt Collins worked on many of our high profile and award winning projects, Riverside Centre, Darling Park, The Anchorage, Penrith Plaza and others. They sold us on the importance of planning and landscape and the added value that they could bring to the project.

What follows are selected examples of the firm's work in this very important area of landscape architecture.

URBAN SPACES

1

2

RIVERSIDE CENTRE

Brisbane, Queensland, Australia

Client
Lend Lease

In the very center of the city, planners at one time proposed a highway fronting the Brisbane River in Queensland, Australia. Lend Lease and its team of designers, however, had other ideas and urged the City of Brisbane to consider alternative proposals. Thus in the early 1980s, Belt Collins worked with Lend Lease, and architect Harry Seidler, on a total urban concept for a portion of the waterfront. That concept has become Riverside Centre, a prestigious office tower development in the city's commercial center.

Anchoring the project is a 3.5-acre landscape design that includes major plaza spaces, a riverfront promenade, rooftop gardens and a major connection from the waterway activities to the hub of the commercial activities in downtown Brisbane.

In the early discussions of the landscape plan, the clients said they wanted a heroic tree as the centerpiece for the plaza. Belt Collins was able to find a 20-meter ficus tree some distance up river. At the time, no tree of that size had ever been transplanted in Australia. The huge tree simply could not be moved over land. The solution was to build a special barge, which floated the tree down river to the plaza where it was craned into place.

Riverside Centre was the first major development to address itself to the river with a ferry landing and riverside promenade. Twenty years later, the entire riverfront is connected with a promenade, river ferries and other riverside activities from the Storey Bridge to the Brisbane Botanic Gardens, a distance of several miles.

Today Riverside Centre forms the heart of the city's financial district. It is said that the plaza has etched itself into Brisbane life, forming the well-attended Sunday Riverside Market, while during the week it provides a vibrant setting for outdoor relaxation by city workers and visitors.

1   Aerial of initial Riverside Tower.
2   Ferry landing adjacent to shoreline promenade.
3   Cascading waterfall and stairway to main plaza.
4   Sweeping forms of landscaped plaza.

3

4

5

6

5 Shoreline promenade with Storey Bridge in background.
6 Aerial view of promenade showing weekend flea market.
7 Night view of stairs leading from water to main plaza.

I have long been an admirer of the work of Belt Collins.

Stuart Hornery, Chairman and CEO of Lend Lease from 1978 to 2000.

7

1

2

3

SAN VITORES BOULEVARD

Tumon Bay, Guam

Client
Government of Guam

1 Renovation of the boulevard has allowed for easy circulation of pedestrians and vehicles.
2 The boulevard before Belt Collins transformation.
3 Planted medians create shade and color.
4 Traffic moves easily after transformation.

Tumon Bay, with its gracefully curving white sand beach, is clearly Guam's prime resort destination area in an urban setting. Along this strand can be found the island's major resort hotels, restaurants, upscale shops and larger shopping complexes.

San Vitores Boulevard, the road connecting all this tourism activity, however, had not kept pace with the glamour of the hotels and other facilities. The area was problematic: enormous concrete poles and utility lines interrupted view planes; there was a lack of trees; extensive, uninterrupted paving, indiscriminate and frequent driveways and curb cuts, and a lack of sidewalks created a general feeling of harshness.

The government of Guam saw an opportunity to change all that with an aim to increase the socioeconomic vitality of the prime Tumon Bay district.

As a first step Belt Collins convinced the government to underground the utilities and to deal with other utilitarian issues, such as proper drainage. Work then began on a promenade that provides comfortable places with shade so people can sit and watch the passing parade, where views to the ocean and parks have been opened up and where pedestrians and vehicles can circulate easily. In the end, the street has become a real boulevard with a much friendlier atmosphere for strollers, outdoor café users and shoppers, which has allowed for a very successful commercial venture.

Work on San Vitores Boulevard started in 1995. Belt Collins continues on the final phase of this extensive project.

4

5

6

7

9

5&7 New sidewalks encourage strolling and visiting.
6 New light poles and underground utilities replaced a
jumble of utilities along the boulevard.
8 Shade is important in tropical climates such as Guam.
9 Before transformation.
10 Landscaping complements the existing buildings.

8

10

1

2

1   Pool deck view from shading trellis.
2   Sun-ray pool pattern provides interest and
    character when viewed from upper units.
3   Calming oasis atmosphere at pool deck.
4   Meandering path creates visual illusion
    and surprise.
5   Curving trellis with climbing vine and
    integrated water feature.
6   Variety of garden views around pool deck.

3

EMPORIUM SUITES

Bangkok, Thailand

Client
City Realty Co., Ltd.

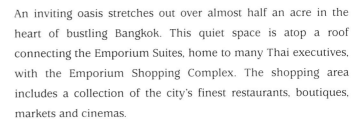

4

An inviting oasis stretches out over almost half an acre in the heart of bustling Bangkok. This quiet space is atop a roof connecting the Emporium Suites, home to many Thai executives, with the Emporium Shopping Complex. The shopping area includes a collection of the city's finest restaurants, boutiques, markets and cinemas.

The rooftop space that Belt Collins designers had to work with included two large spaces at different levels connected by a narrower space interrupted by a large skylight.

The solution was to design a restful, circular Skygarden at the higher and larger end. Included are a multi-purpose family lawn, many flowering trees and two round quiet gardens that are separated from the main lawn. At the edge of the Skygarden is a tiered, hanging garden that reaches down to the next level, as well as a graceful waterfall. At the other, lower end is the main pool with a striking sun ray design embedded in the pool surface.

Circulation between the two main areas is enhanced via a meandering walkway that passes through a wild tropical garden.

5

6

1

1 Bird's eye view of main plaza and water feature.
2 Patterns and shapes.
3 View from Darling Park Building lobby into plaza.
4 Detail of bronze waterfowl that adorn the water feature.

2

DARLING PARK
Sydney, Australia

Client
Lend Lease

A show called *Gardening Australia* that reported on Darling Park said it best: 'In Sydney, like any large city, life gets busier and busier, with an ever increasing volume of traffic, more freeways, not to mention people. Green space is at a premium'.

Darling Park is a massive five-building project that was built in the airspace above five roadways. Among the components of the project are 75,000 square feet of office space, a 10,000 square-foot shopping complex and a 100-room hotel. Belt Collins worked with two architectural firms to create a landscaped oasis that has become an important open space in one of the central business district's busiest precincts.

The design was a specialized 'on structure' installation with mature trees transplanted into the plaza space. This formed an outdoor café, which featured a billabong-themed water sculpture. Robust planted areas soften and provide color to the paved terrace. The plaza also acts as a pedestrian transition space from downtown Sydney to the waterfront of Darling Park.

Gardening Australia also reported that 'the garden was designed for recreation use and is frequented by nearby office workers for lunch or tea breaks...these small areas are often used by business people, clinching a deal in surroundings much more conducive to clear thinking than bustling offices'.

This was another successful collaboration with one of Australia's premier architects, Harry Seidler. The civic space design was a collaboration with architect Eric Kuhne.

3

4

ABERDEEN MARINA
Hong Kong

Client
Kerry Properties

1   The pool area provides a sanctuary in busy Hong Kong.
2   Boats docked at Aberdeen Marina.
3   Aberdeen site before development.

Those who have visited or done business in Hong Kong know well the hustle and bustle of this famed city. Highrises march, in row after row. Car traffic and foot traffic can be chaotic to say the least.

Even in the old Aberdeen district, 2,000 fishing junks would jostle for dock space so that they could peddle their wares. But because land is a precious commodity in this part of the world, it became apparent all of that would have to change.

Belt Collins was engaged to transform the shoreline area through an evolving master plan into a marina offering great respite. Nowadays members of the Marina Club can park their cars, berth their yachts, swim in sparkling pools, play tennis and get a workout where before thousands of fishmongers plied their trade.

The firm's designers carried the water theme through the entire project by sculpting as a centerpiece a handsome rooftop 20-meter pool for races and leisure swimming. In recognition of making precious space work as hard as possible, a daytime children's pool changes at night into a reflecting pool with fountains.

2

3

4

5

4,5&7   Popular freeform pool complete with
        waterfalls and slides built over the water.
   6   Original rooftop pool

6

7

1

1   Interior landscape of arrival and departure hall.
2&3   Seamless transition from exterior to interior landscape.

2

BRISBANE INTERNATIONAL AIRPORT
NEW TERMINAL COMPLEX
Brisbane, Australia

Client
Civil and Civic

Brisbane Airport is considered a major tourist entry into Australia. As such, it was felt that the airport space should make a unique statement about the geographic area.

The concept Belt Collins developed entailed creating a 'snapshot' of the Queensland landscape by incorporating as many of the region's signature species as possible, both native and exotic.

What distinguishes the landscape design is the full integration of interior and exterior spaces. The project site was comprised totally of reclaimed sand that presented many horticultural challenges. Rather than removing the large amount of surface material, Belt Collins' solution was to utilize sand displaced during building construction and sculpt the otherwise flat landscape to emulate the rolling dune forms of the Queensland coastline.

Internally, mature native palms and fig trees were planted to reinforce the integration of external and internal spaces, a concept exemplified in vernacular Queensland architecture. This took place only after extensive acclimatization and studies for plant health lighting requirements.

One of the features of the site is the Photo Opportunity Plaza, which includes a display of four mature Queensland Bottle Trees transplanted from a western farm property.

3

4

5

6

4 Interior atrium creates feeling of being in a garden.
5 Interior water feature.
6 Overview of landscaped car park with mass transit in background.
7 Queensland bottle tree provides backdrop for photo opportunity.
8 Roadside planting along entry drive screens the adjacent car park.

7

8

1

3

1 Sculptural water spouts align the shallow
  water feature.
2 Detail of water spout.
3 Steps leading to the main grand podium.
4 Looking into plaza showing composition of
  planting and paving.
5 View of plaza from the adjacent street
  showing entrance water feature.

GRAND MILLENNIUM PLAZA

Hong Kong

Client
Urban Renewal Authority

4

Belt Collins prepared the landscape master plan for this 2,100-square-meter mixed-use urban renewal project, which includes office and retail space. In recognition of the site's partialy European heritage, the firm's detailed design for the plaza incorporated an Italian piazza theme in the public open spaces.

The landscape design also complements the architecture of the surrounding buildings. Curving stairways set amongst water features reach various levels of the plaza. The theme is further brought to life with special lighting features and a unique monumental bronze fountain.

One of the highlights of the plaza is a large 24-point sunburst that welcomes pedestrians from the street.

5

Other Significant Belt Collins Urban Projects:

Hawai'i State Capitol, Honolulu, Hawai'i, USA

Pacific Place, Hong Kong

Plaza 138, Kuala Lumpur, Malaysia

The Centre, Hong Kong

Surfers Paradise Revitalization, Queensland, Australia

Jiangbei New Town, Chongqing, China

1

2

1 Hawai'i State Capitol designed as volcanic form arising from ocean-like reflecting pools and open lawn areas.
2 Jiangbei New Town in China being built as a result of flooding the Yangtze River.
3 The Centre gardens offer green space among high-rises in Hong Kong.
4 Pedestrian mall within six-acre urban complex at Pacific Place in Hong Kong.
5 Surfers Paradise in Australia where several core streets were revitalized.

4

3

5

Belt Collins has provided master planning and landscape architectural design for entire new towns, high-rise condominium complexes, mixed-use projects, and resort and residential properties. The firm is involved continually with the transformation of derelict and under-utilized sites into highly productive economic properties.

Bob Donovan, formerly Vice President of Construction and Development for the Lana'i Company in Hawai'i and now Executive Vice President and Chief Operating Officer of The Ford Plantation in Georgia, said of Belt Collins,

For more than 30 years, I have worked on high-end residential land development projects. In that time, I have worked with leading landscape architecture, land planning and engineering firms in the country. Belt Collins understands land development and engineering better than anyone. Their professional staff is highly knowledgeable about land development issues and has the design ability to deal with difficult sites and infrastructure issues in a beautiful and sensitive way. They sold us on the integration of planning, landscape architecture and engineering and the added value they bring to the project.

What follows are several examples among the hundreds of residential projects completed by Belt Collins.

RESIDENTIAL PROJECTS

The Villas at Koele

Belt Collins understands land development and engineering better than anyone.

Bob Donovan, formerly Vice President of Construction and Development for the Lana'i Company in Hawai'i and now Executive Vice President and Chief Operating Officer of The Ford Plantation in Georgia.

1

2

3

4

5

KUALA KENCANA NEW TOWN

West Papua, Indonesia

Client
PT Freeport Indonesia

6

7

It isn't often that landscape architects are challenged to create an entirely new town on over 1,500 acres, but that was exactly the situation for the firm's professionals when they were assigned to design the landscape master plan for the town of Kuala Kencana in the Timika region of West Papua, Indonesia.

This new town, with an initial population of 9,000, was planned to provide housing and other support amenities for the nearby Freeport Gold and Copper Mine.

The biggest challenge for the designers was the location of the new town in the lowland rainforest of West Papua. This is a fragile ecosystem, which required very careful site planning and close attention to ecological issues by Belt Collins. Going to great lengths, the firm developed detailed criteria to decide which trees could stay and which would have to be felled. Those felled were used in constructing decking, bridges and boardwalks, all of which were elevated above the rainforest floor, thus retaining intact the flora, fauna, soil profile and water drainage systems of the lowland rainforest ecosystem.

Besides those mentioned, the firm took many other steps to be ecologically, environmentally and culturally sensitive such as developing a special nursery to propagate the unique flora of the region for use on the project. Belt Collins designed a dramatic entry with five traditional totems over 10 meters high, which were hand-carved on the site by a team of local Komoro woodcarvers.

Besides housing, the Kuala Kencana master plan also provided its inhabitants with recreational facilities, services that include stores, banks, a post office, library and telecommunications, light industrial areas and other amenities such as schools and places of worship.

1   The lowland rainforest environment at Kuala Kencana.
2   Timber bollard being carved by a local craftsman.
3   Monumental Komoro totems were used as a dramatic entry feature to the new town.
4   Residential area.
5   Community amenities.
6   New town during construction in the lowland rainforest.
7   A mosque is one of several places of worship.

1

2

TANGLIN VIEW CONDOMINIUM

Singapore

Client
Far East Organisation

1 Rest pavilion amidst bubbler jets.
2 Main pool and fun pool united by the reflection of arching jets.
3&4 Night and day views of main entry porte cochere.

The Belt Collins landscape architects for this high-rise condominium decided from the beginning that the project needed a highly individual character to set it apart from all other developments in Singapore, as well as public housing across the street.

Their concept was to create a Mondrian-like sculpted landscape based on the Dutch painter's balance of verticals and horizontals, with no curves and no diagonals. Using walls with openings cut out, vertical arbors and horizontal arbor elements overhead, a series of loosely defined garden 'rooms' were created. These personalized garden niches can be used for sitting quietly with a book or chatting with a companion.

Water is the central element of the design. The pivotal recreational amenity is a 45-meter main pool for swimming laps. There is also a fun pool with arching jets, rain curtains and bubble mats; a jet fun pool with a grid of vertical water jets; a children's pool with gentle, arching water jets; and a Jacuzzi with therapeutic jets. Parts of the fun pool and the children's pool are beneath arbors that encourage lounging in the water.

3

4

5

6

7

8

9

5 Overall view of pool area from residential unit.
6 Fun pool with arching jets.
7 Stepped cascade at main swimming pool.
8 Modernism in the primordial jungle.
9 Contrasting form and color.
10 Swimming pool entry steps.
11 Main entry water feature and signage.

10

11

1&2   Distinctive white rail fences delineate private ranches.
  3   Access was designed to emulate early ranch roads.
4&5   Many live as permanent residents while others find the
       location ideal as a second home.
  6   Upper entry to the ranch.

1

2

3

4

KOHALA RANCH

Island of Hawai'i, USA

Client
Kohala Ranch

5

6

Kohala Ranch was at one time part of an ancient *ahupua'a*, which is a uniquely Hawaiian land division. Typically an *ahupua'a* reached from the mountaintop down to the ocean in a large wedge shape. Early Hawaiian kings awarded these land divisions to their prime chiefs so their villagers could have access to fresh water and forest resources at higher elevations, land to grow sweet potatoes and other crops in the midlands and an ability to harvest the bounty of the sea at the shoreline. In fact, each *ahupua'a* was a model of self-sufficiency and sustainability.

Kohala Ranch, which is a 4,000-acre planned residential community of three, five and ten-acre private ranches, is essentially based on two of these *ahupua'a*. In all of its services provided to this client—physical and environmental planning, civil engineering, landscape architecture and golf course design—the firm showed sensitivity to the cultural history of the area.

As an example, great care was taken in designing the water system, which was a challenge due to the large land area and the extreme changes in elevation, ranging from 3,000 feet at the upper reaches to 120 feet near the ocean. A distinctive design feature is a simple white rail fence that lines the coastal highway and mountain road entrances as well as enclosing the private ranches.

Today Kohala Ranch is a very successful rural community that offers an alternative to urban living. Plans call for additional recreational and residential amenities, including a 27-hole golf course, equestrian trails and center, shopping village and other community facilities.

1

2

1 Anchorage Phase One residential and marina development.
2 Residential streetscape.
3 Marina boardwalk/promenade.
4 Transitional landscape between marina and residential.
5 Aerial of project midway during development.

3

THE ANCHORAGE

New South Wales, Australia

Client
Lend Lease

Starting in 1980, Belt Collins has assisted with eight phases of this 750-unit residential project on the spectacular Gold Coast of Australia. The Anchorage at Tweed Heads is located on a man-made marina at a sandbar in the mouth of the Tweed River.

In developing the master plan, the client wanted to break away from the existing pattern of previous waterfront developments along the Gold Coast, with their finger-like, grid-shaped design. Working with Lend Lease Design's principal architect, Ross Bonthorne, the firm's solution was to design a more natural, curvilinear design, reflective of the best attributes of the natural environment.

The Anchorage is a medium density development with no structures higher than a palm tree. In addition, certain design principles were developed that include creating, directing and framing views; establishing appropriate settings for various types of development; and establishing the relationship of building masses to the scale of the landscape. A key part of the overall plan was to develop the entire shoreline area as a public reserve with trails, picnic areas, places for shoreline fishing and public access to the river environment.

In describing why Belt Collins was chosen for this project, the owners/developers Lend Lease and Civil/Civic said, 'their brilliant use of the tropical and sub-tropical vegetation has touched nearly every major garden environment in the Pacific'.

4

5

1   Overall view of golf course and future residential lots.
2&3 View of golf frontage housing showing retained
     existing trees and watercourse.
4   View of golf course with mountains in the
     background.
5   Golf frontage housing.

TAMAN DAYU

Indonesia

Client
PT HM Sampoerna

4

5

This 2,000-unit residential/resort community high in the cool mountains of East Java is one of the best examples of Belt Collins' ability to integrate master planning, engineering and landscape architecture.

The integration was vital because in the first instance the area was environmentally sensitive, surrounded by rice paddies, villages and rain forests. Different cultural influences such as Feng Shui (a belief that all things should be in proper balance) and Numerology (a belief that certain numbers are lucky while others are bad luck) had to be honored.

Existing streams were retained and used as part of the site drainage system. Also retained were existing mature kapok trees and rice fields that became part of the working agricultural system within the master plan.

The Belt Collins planners, engineers, and landscape architects had been faced with similar demands many times before, which was precisely why the firm was hired for this massive project. The Taman Dayu project demonstrates the advantages of integrating many skill areas from one company, so that in the end all aspects function smoothly and are harmonious.

The result is a wondrous, mixed-use property, with villas surrounded by rice terraces and amenities including village shops, a water park and the golf clubhouse. The Jack Nicklaus Golf Course meanders through the landscape, and roads meander like ribbons of open space through the project.

6   Private swimming pool adjacent to golf course.
7   View of Taman Dayu clubhouse.
8&9   Views of golf course where existing river, trees and
      rice terraces were retained.
10   Housing along the golf course.

6

7

8

10

9

1

1   Cascade wall.
2   Custom designed lanterns create unique identity along
    riverside promenade.
3   Formal tree lined waterway promenade.
4   Featured fish motif sculptures along neighborhood path.

2

STAR RIVER
Panyu (Guangzhou), China

Client
Guangzhou Hongfu Real Estate Co., Inc.

Belt Collins' focus on innovative landscape design is clearly evident throughout this large-scale development which hugs the Pearl River in Southern China. That focus is well demonstrated in a landscape design that provides a refreshing perspective on residential developments in China.

Tropical sub-themes such as Mexican, Polynesian, Californian and Spanish were introduced to create a unique identity for each of Star River's residential districts. These districts were then seamlessly connected via artfully flowing pathways. Another notable landscape element is a nearly half-mile timber boardwalk cantilevered over the adjacent Pearl River.

Reinforcing the landscape theme is the extensive use of water features. Water in every imaginable form can be seen, heard and experienced within major vantage points of the project. One observer said that the landscape design is truly a celebration of water.

Students from the local university closely followed Belt Collins' sketches to construct numerous tropical-style hand-carved sandstone relief panels and innovative bronze and marble sculptural creations placed strategically throughout the landscape.

3

4

5

6

7

8

5 Harmonious landscape blends multiple forms, colors
   and textures.
6 Distinctive main entrance landscape.
7 Gentle cascade produces the soothing sound of falling
   water. A pond full of colorful koi within clubhouse area.
8 Water walkway.
9 Decorative wall highlights a portion of the garden.

9

2

1

1 Scenic view of stone seating in pavilion set amongst the rich tiered landscape of the podium garden.
2 Aerial view of the Roman Plaza atop the car park.
3 Gazebo plant-pattern roof.
4 Grand Roman style landscape with stepped water feature and royal archways.
5 Walkway through structured podium landscape gardens.

3

COVE PENINSULA

Shenzhen, Guangdong, China

Client
Shenzhen Bandao Real Estate
Development Co., Inc.

Because this residential project is located in the suburb of Shekou, west of the city of Shenzhen, the owners were searching for something to attract urban buyers.

As a large-scale project with 12 ten-story towers in the first phase and 15 mid-rise towers and a 26-story high-rise tower in the second phase, the client engaged Belt Collins to design a varied landscape with different characteristics of diverse identities.

For the Roman Plaza, atop the residents' car park, the firm designed a classical, geometric composition. This formality plays an important part in the floorscape, water fountains with cascades and other architectural elements.

As a change of pace, the firm designed a Resort Zone with meandering footpaths, undulating mounds, organic swales of planting and fluid edges of water bodies to provide residents the opportunity to enjoy a natural ambience in the comfort of their own homes.

For those residents whose entrance is located on the upper level, which is somewhat removed from the main landscape environment, the firm designed a Garden in the Sky. The intermediate spaces were used to create lushly planted courtyards, ideal for elderly residents.

4 5

6   Large granite spheres simplistically define
    the waterway edge within the landscape
    garden.
7&8 Views of the simple lakeside walkway
    with complementary planting.
9–11 Structured hard and softscape form the
    walkway environment.

6

7

8

9

11

10

1 Entry fountain and roundabout with arrival pavilion in background.
2 The arrival pavilion and two matching water pavilions serve as visual anchors for the overall landscape.
3 Night view of axial to main swimming pool.
4 Night view of entry roundabout with arrival pavilion beyond.
5 Night view of fun pool and water pavilion.

2

1

3

HERITAGE VIEW CONDOMINIUM

Singapore

Client
Far East Organisation

4

The landscape for Heritage View Condominium creates a quality lifestyle environment of an international caliber. Sweeping gestures using quality finishes create the sense that residents are living in a five-star enclave.

On arrival, visitors and residents alike experience a country club-like entrance drive paralleled by an impressive wall fountain. At the end of the drive the landscape explodes into an impressive arrival court. At its center is an elegantly woven pattern of granite pavers ringed by manicured plantings. Surrounding this is a ring fountain with multiple jets arcing toward and welcoming both residents and guests.

The main swimming pool and clubhouse terrace are the focus of the leisure environment. Sitting in the main pool, the centerpiece of Heritage View is a 10-meter tall sculptural fountain composed of a trio of vertical elements. Water spirals and cascades down from the top of these elements into the pool, creating a graceful and dynamic display. The central focus of these three pools is an 11.5-meter tall pavilion with multiple streams of water falling from two pools and a bridge piercing the third. This unique ring pool encircles a palm-filled landscape that surrounds the main pool.

5

Other Significant Belt Collins Residential Projects:

Villas at Koele, Lana'i, Hawai'i, USA

Hillsborough Court, Hong Kong

Pacific Plaza Towers, Fort Bonifacio, Philippines

Dynasty Court, Shenzhen, China

Bangkok Garden, Bangkok, Thailand

Visto Paradiso, Hong Kong

Bayshore Condominium, Singapore

Manele Terraces, Lana'i, Hawai'i, USA

1

2

3

1 The Villas at Koele on the golf course, Lana'i, Hawai'i.
2 Water-feature at Hillsborough Court, Hong Kong.
3 Manele Terraces overlook the ocean, Lana'i, Hawai'i.
4 Dialogue of formal and organic garden at Bangkok
  Garden in Thailand.

4

5

6

7

5 Landscape softens Pacific Plaza Towers, Philippines.
6 Landscape enhances Dynasty Court, Shenzhen, China.
7 Garden designed to be seen from above as well as at ground
   level at Visto Paradiso, Hong Kong.
8 Bird's eye view of pool at Bayshore Condominium, Singapore.

8

WORLDWIDE OFFICES

Honolulu

Anne Mapes, President, Belt Collins Hawaii

2153 North King Street, Suite 200

Honolulu, Hawai'i 96819-4554 USA

Tel: 808 521-5361

Fax: 808 538-7819

E-mail: honolulu@beltcollins.com

Seattle

Peter Geyer, President, Belt Collins Seattle

Nautical Landing Marina

2500 Westlake Avenue North, Suite G

Seattle, Washington 98109 USA

Tel: 206 285-4422

Fax: 206 285-0644

E-mail: seattle@beltcollins.com

Hong Kong

Anthony Hui, President and Managing Director,

Belt Collins Hong Kong

20th Floor, Dominion Centre

43 Queen's Road East

Wanchai, Hong Kong

Tel: 852 2528-9233

Fax: 852 2520-0878

E-mail: hongkong@beltcollins.com

Singapore

Allen Kerton, Managing Director, Belt Collins Singapore

No. 4 & 6 Ann Siang Hill

Singapore 069786

Tel: 65 6223-8133

Fax: 65 6222-9602

E-mail: singapore@beltcollins.com

Thailand

Somwong Leevanijkul, Managing Director, Belt Collins Thailand

73/9, Soi Ruam Rudee 2

Phloenchit Road

Lumpini, Pathumwan

Bangkok 10330 Thailand

Tel: 662 254-1001

Fax: 662 254-1006

E-mail: thailand@beltcollins.com

Guam

Elizabeth Gayle, Vice President/Manager, Belt Collins Guam

GCIC Building, Suite 209

414 West Soledad Avenue

Hagåtña, Guam 96910 USA

Tel: 671 477-6148

Fax: 671 472-4969

E-mail: guam@beltcollins.com

FIRM PROFILE

SERVICES

Robert Belt was a civil engineer and Walter Collins a land planner. The firm started with those two services and, in the very early days in Hawai'i, that was how the company gained its reputation for excellence. As more public and private clients came to the firm, demand grew for a greater range of services from Belt Collins. This is how the comprehensive range of disciplines listed below developed.

Landscape Architecture

Landscape Master Plans

Resort Environment Planning

Parks, Recreation, and Open Space Planning and Design

Golf Course Design and Landscape Design

Exterior Hardscape Design

Water Feature Planning and Design

Planting and Irrigation Design

Landscape Maintenance and Remedial Programming

Landscape Lighting Design

Streetscapes

Planning

Land Use Studies

Master Plans and Site Plans

Regional and Community Plans

Subdivision Plans

Permit Applications and Documentation

Resort Planning

Urban Design

Massing Studies for Buildings

Urban Space Analysis

Land Reclamation Planning

Zoning Analysis

Due Diligence Studies

Land Taking Studies

Circulation and Shadow Studies

Expert Witness Services

Security Site Planning

Computer Services/Graphics

Computer Aided Design and Drafting (CADD)

Electronic Data File Transfer and Conversion

Plotting, Digitizing, and Scanning

Geographic Information Systems (GIS)

Software Application Training

Computer Imaging

Public Meeting Graphics

Computer Generated Graphics

Report Graphics

Brochures and Annual Reports

Civil/Sanitary Engineering

Feasibility Studies

Infrastructure Master Plans

Site Engineering

Roadway Design

Traffic and Transportation Engineering

Drainage and Flood Control Studies

Coastal Engineering

Sanitary Engineering

Wastewater Facilities Studies and Master Plans

Wastewater Facilities Siting and Design

Sanitary Landfill Siting and Design

Environmental Consulting

Environmental Impact Statements

Environmental Assessments

Soil and Groundwater Contamination Investigations

Air and Water Quality Evaluations

Integrated Cultural and Natural Resources Management Plans

Storm Water Discharge Monitoring and Permitting

Environmental Site Assessments for Real Estate Transactions

Solid and Hazardous Waste Disposal Permits

Pollution Prevention and Integrated Solid Waste Management Plans

1971 Belt Collins merged with Lyon Associates.

1975 Initially opened the Hong Kong office to master plan Discovery Bay. The Hong Kong office has since grown to over 225 employees with a diverse staff from ten countries.

1953 Founded by Robert M. Belt and Walter K. Collins as a civil engineering and planning firm. The firm redesigned sugar cane haul roads for C. Brewer & Co. on Hawai'i, which was the firm's first client.

1962 Began work on Mauna Kea Beach Resort with Laurance S. Rockefeller. Belt Collins provided site and master planning, landscape architecture and civil engineering as well as regional water and road systems design. The firm gained golf course design expertise working with Robert Trent Jones Sr.

1963 Landscape architecture added as a staffed department of the firm.

1980 First golf course designed solely by the firm at Mauna Lani Resort where Belt Collins also provided master planning, civil engineering, landscape architecture and environmental consulting.

1961–1970

1953–1960

1955 Produced the Ka'anapali Beach Resort Master Plan on Maui, the first of its kind in the world. Seven hotels, two golf courses, a shopping center and several condominium projects were developed under the plan.

1960 A main contributor to the State of Hawai'i Visitor Destination Study. This type of tourism planning study was accomplished by Belt Collins and served as a prototype for many other countries and regions leading to the development of numerous world-class destination resorts throughout the Pacific. Hawai'i today is recognized as the mecca of tourism development.

1964 Opened first overseas office in Bangkok, Thailand as a joint venture called Belt Lemmon & Lo. The JV provided a range of capabilities including architecture, mechanical, electrical and structural engineering, in addition to Belt Collins' master planning, landscape architecture and civil engineering.

1969 For the government of Singapore, created a plan for Sentosa Island. Originally planned as a recreation resort for the people of Singapore, it has become a major visitor destination.

1971–1981

1981 Belt Collins name and assets purchased from Lyon Associates by five veteran Belt Collins employees representing the firm's major disciplines: Joe Vierra, Ray Cain, Paul Hirota, Tom Papandrew and Jim Bell.

1982 Opened Singapore office as a result of the boom in development in Singapore, India, Malaysia and Indonesia.

1983 Provided landscape architecture for Tanjong Jara Beach Hotel and Rantau Abang Visitors' Centre as a result of preparing a major Visitor Destination Study for the Malaysian government. This project won the prestigious Aga Khan Award.

1982–1994

MILESTONES

1987 Award of Excellence given to Belt Collins by the Urban Land Institute for large scale recreational development at the Mauna Kea Beach Resort on the Big Island of Hawai'i.

1990s Began a transition of ownership from the five who repurchased Belt Collins in 1981 to a much wider group of employee/owners to assure succession.

1993 In all of its worldwide offices, Belt Collins reached 10,000 built projects. This same year the firm added Environmental Consulting Services and opened its Guam office.

1995 Anne Mapes was named president of Belt Collins Hawaii Ltd., the first female to head that company.

1996 The Consulting Engineers Council of Hawaii awarded Belt Collins its Grand Conceptor award for Lanai City Auxiliary Wastewater Treatment Facility, culminating over 100 national and international engineering awards since the firm's founding in 1953.

1997 The firm opened its Seattle office.

1995–2003

1999 Urban land Institute Award of Excellence given to the firm for large-scale recreational development at Hualalai Four Seasons Resort on the Big Island of Hawai'i. The State of Hawai'i honored Belt Collins with the Governor's Exporter of the Year Award.

2000 In Guangzhou, China, started the ongoing landscape design for the large-scale Star River residential project, which is one of more than 100 projects the firm has worked on throughout China.

2003 Belt Collins celebrates its 50th year with over 350 employees in seven offices around the world.

BeltCollins

50
1953-2003
YEARS OF
EXCELLENCE

Projects for which Belt Collins has provided design or consulting services have received over 250 national and international awards since the firm's founding in 1953. Ranging from landscape design for small public playgrounds to master-planning and site-work engineering for major destination resorts, these award-winning projects and their respective awards are shown below.

AWARDS

1

2

3

2002 Pilot Study on the Use of Contaminated Dredged Material, Oahu, Hawai'i
American Council of Engineering Companies of Hawaii, Honor Award

2002 The Gold Coast, South Kohala/North Kona, Hawai'i
American Planning Association, Hawaii Chapter, Donald Wolbrink Chapter Achievement Award

2002 Heritage View, Singapore [1]
Construction Excellence Award

2002 Seasons View, Singapore
Construction Excellence Award (Merit)

2002 Tanglin View, Singapore [2]
Construction Industry Development Board (CIDB), BCA Best Buildable Design Award

2002 Gardenville, Singapore
Construction Industry Development Board (CIDB), BCA Construction Excellence (Merit) Award (Residential Building)

2002 House of Tan Yeok Nee/University of Chicago Graduate School of Business, Singapore
FIABCI Prix d'Excellence Award

2002 Gardenville, Singapore
FIABCI Prix d'Excellence Award (Residential Building)

2002 Ford Island Development Communication Program, Pearl Harbor, Hawai'i
International Association of Business Communicators Hawaii Chapter, Ilima Award of Merit

2002 Yin Hai Forest, Kunming, China
Orient Landscape Design, Ecological and Environmental Excellence Award, CIHAF

2002 Ford Island Development Communication Program, Pearl Harbor, Hawai'i
Public Relations Society of America Hawaii Chapter, Koa Anvil Award

2001 Pearl Harbor Historic Trail, Oahu, Hawai'i
American Planning Association, Hawaii Chapter, Community-Based Planning Award

2001 Poipu Bridge Replacement, Ho'onani Road, Koloa, Hawai'i
American Public Works Association Hawaii Chapter, Project of the Year

2001 Honolulu Academy of Arts Luce Pavilion, Honolulu, Hawai'i
Building Industry Association of Hawaii, Renaissance Building & Remodeling Award

2001 Trellis Towers, Singapore
Construction Industry Development Board (CIDB), BCA Best Buildable Design Awards (Residential Building)

2001 Woodsvale, Singapore
Construction Industry Development Board (CIDB), BCA Best Buildable Design Awards (Residential Building)

2001 Grand Hotel d'Angkor, Siem Reap, Cambodia [3]
Construction Industry Development Board (CIDB), BCA Construction Excellence Awards (Commercial Building)

2001 King's Centre/Grand Copthorne Waterfront Hotel, Singapore
Construction Industry Development Board (CIDB), BCA Construction Excellence Awards (Commercial Building)

2001 Parc Palais, Singapore
Construction Industry Development Board (CIDB), BCA Construction Excellence Awards (Residential Building)

2001 Waipio Soccer Complex, Waipahu, Hawai'i
Consulting Engineers Council of Hawaii, Honor Award

2001 The Andaman, Datai Bay, Langkawi, Malaysia
FIABCI (Malaysia Chapter), Award of Distinction for Resort Development

2001 The Shangri-La Hotel, Singapore
Garden City Awards (Hotel)

2001 East Point Green, Singapore
Garden City Awards (Private Residential)

2001 **Gardenville, Singapore**
Garden City Awards (Private Residential)

2001 **Orchard Parksuites, Singapore**
Garden City Awards (Private Residential)

2001 **Yin Hai Shan Shui Jian, Kunming, China**
Orient Landscape Design, Community Landscape Design Award, CIHAF

2001 **The Andaman, Datai Bay, Langkawi, Malaysia** [4]
Pacific Asia Travel Association, Gold Award, Environmental Education Program

2001 **House of Tan Yeok Nee/University of Chicago Graduate School of Business, Singapore**
Singapore Heritage Award

2000 **Kealakekua Bay State Historical Park Conceptual Plan, Napo'opo'o, Hawai'i**
American Planning Association, Hawaii Chapter, Environment/Preservation Award

2000 **University of Hawaii at Manoa Athletic Practice Fields, Honolulu, Hawai'i**
Consulting Engineers Council of Hawaii, Honor Award

2000 **Battleship Missouri Memorial, Pearl Harbor, Hawai'i**
Historic Hawaii Foundation, Governor's Preservation Award

2000 **Battleship Missouri Memorial, Pearl Harbor, Hawai'i**
National Preservation Honor Award

2000 **Vanova, Beijing, China**
National Residential Landscape for Conceptual Design, Gold Medal Award

2000 **The Centre, Hong Kong, China**
Outstanding Green Project Awards, Silver Award–Landscape Design

2000 **The Andaman, Datai Bay, Langkawi, Malaysia**
Pacific Asia Travel Association, Grand Award, Environmental Conservation

1999 **Ka'upulehu Integrated Resources Management Plan, Kona, Hawai'i**
American Planning Association, Hawaii Chapter, Environment/Preservation Award

1999 **Grand Hotel d'Angkor, Siem Reap, Cambodia**
British Airways 'Tourism for Tomorrow' Award

1999 **Banyan Tree Resort, Phuket, Thailand** [5]
Condé Nast Traveler, 1999 Eco-Tourism Award

1999 **The Bayshore, Singapore**
Construction Industry Development Board (CIDB), BCA Construction Excellence Award (Residential Building)

1999 **Ala Wai Canal Dredging Conceptual Design and Environmental Assessment, Honolulu, Hawai'i**
Consulting Engineers Council of Hawaii, Honor Award

1999 **Battleship Missouri Memorial, Pearl Harbor, Hawai'i**
Consulting Engineers Council of Hawaii, Honor Award

1999 **The Bayshore, Singapore**
FIABCI Prix d'Excellence Award (Residential Building)

1999 **Grand Millennium Plaza, Hong Kong, China**
Green Project Award, Certification of Merit–Landscape Design

1999 **Shangri-La's Rasa Ria Resort, Kota Kinabalu, Malaysia**
Sabah's Best Resort Landscaping Award

1999 **Avillion Village Resort, Port Dickson, Malaysia**
State of Negeri Sembilan, Best (1st Place) Landscape

1999 **Hualalai at Historic Ka'upulehu, Kona, Hawai'i** [6]
Urban Land Institute (ULI), Award for Excellence, Recreational Large-Scale

4

5

6

7

8

9

1998 Shangri-La Hotel, Bangkok, Thailand
Business Traveler, Best Business Hotel in Asia

1998 Taman Dayu Residential Resort, Indonesia
Consulting Engineers Council of Hawaii, Honor Award

1998 Surfers Paradise Streetscape, Queensland, Australia [7]
Gold Coast Urban Design, Civic Places Award

1998 Surfers Paradise Streetscape, Queensland, Australia
Gold Coast Urban Design, Gold Award

1998 National Tropical Botanical Garden Visitor Center, Lawa'i, Hawai'i
Historic Hawaii Foundation, Preservation Award

1998 The Andaman, Datai Bay, Langkawi, Malaysia
Malaysian Government, Best Landscaped Hotel Award

1998 Alexandra Beach Family Resort, Queensland, Australia
Maroochy Shire Council's Town Planning Award

1998 Darling Walk/Sega World Complex, Sydney, Australia
Master Builders Association, Excellence in Construction Award for Building–Entertainment/ Hospitality

1998 Polynesian Cultural Center, Alii Luau Garden, La'ie, Hawai'i [8]
National Landscape Association, American Garden Award, Best Commercial Garden Space

1997 Center for Hawaiian Studies, University of Hawai'i, Honolulu, Hawai'i
American Institute of Architects Honolulu Chapter, Award of Merit

1997 Hapuna Beach Prince Hotel, South Kohala, Hawai'i
American Institute of Architects Honolulu Chapter, Award of Merit

1997 Dillingham Hall, Punahou School, Honolulu, Hawai'i
American Institute of Architects, National Honor Award for Interior Design

1997 Brisbane International Airport, New Terminal Complex, Brisbane, Australia
Australian Institute of Landscape Architects, Merit Award

1997 Darling Park, Sydney Australia
Australian Institute of Landscape Architects, Merit Award for Urban & Civic Design

1997 The Bayshore, Singapore
Construction Industry Development Board (CIDB), BCA Best Buildable Design Awards (Residential Building)

1997 Orchard Parksuites, Singapore
Construction Industry Development Board (CIDB), BCA Construction Excellence Awards (Residential Building)

1997 Hualalai at Historic Ka'upulehu, Kona, Hawai'i
Consulting Engineers Council of Hawaii, Honor Award

1997 Hong Kong Temple, Kowloon, Hong Kong, China [9]
Hong Kong Institute of Architects, Certificate of Merit

1997 Sai Sha Residential and Recreational Development, New Territories, Hong Kong, China
Hong Kong Institute of Planners, Silver Medal Award

1997 Hualalai at Historic Ka'upulehu, Kona, Hawai'i
Kona Outdoor Circle Beautification Award

1997 Lana'i City Auxiliary Wastewater Treatment Facility, Lana'i City, Hawai'i
Pacific Asia Travel Association, Green Earth Award

1996 1100 Alakea Plaza, Honolulu, Hawai'i
American Institute of Architects Honolulu Chapter, Award of Merit

1996 Waimea Plantation Cottages, Waimea, Hawai'i
American Institute of Architects Honolulu Chapter, Award of Merit

1996 Lana'i City Auxiliary Wastewater Treatment Facility, Lana'i City, Hawai'i [10]
American Society of Civil Engineers, Hawaii Section, Certificate of Meritorious Achievement

1996 Lana'i City Auxiliary Wastewater Treatment Facility, Lana'i City, Hawai'i
Consulting Engineers Council of Hawaii, Grand Conceptor Award

1996 Taman Dayu Residential Resort, Indonesia [11]
Gripa Cipta Nugraha, Best Master Planned Environmental Development, Suara Indonesia

1996 Pacific Islands Club Guam Expansion, Tumon Bay, Guam [12]
Guam Beautification Award

1996 **Darling Park, Sydney Australia**
Landscape Contractors Association
of New South Wales, Award for
Excellence

1995 **Hawai'i State Capitol, Honolulu,
Hawai'i**
American Institute of Architects
Honolulu Chapter, 25 Year Award

1995 **The Bluffs at Mauna Kea, South
Kohala, Hawai'i**
American Institute of Architects
Honolulu Chapter, Award of Merit

1995 **The Elizabeth Hotel, Singapore**
Construction Industry Development
Board (CIDB), BCA Construction
Excellence Awards (Commercial
Building)

1995 **East Mamala Bay Wastewater
Facilities Plan and Environmental
Impact Statement, Honolulu,
Hawai'i**
Consulting Engineers Council of
Hawaii, Excellence Award

1995 **Dillingham Hall, Punahou School,
Honolulu, Hawai'i**
Consulting Engineers Council of
Hawaii, Grand Conceptor Award

1995 **The Villas at Koele, Lana'i City,
Hawai'i**
Gold Nugget Award, Award of Merit,
Residential Project of the Year

1995 **Sunnyville Estate, Nam Sang Wai,
Hong Kong, China**
Hong Kong Institute of Planners,
Award of Merit for Planning
Proposal

1995 **Mauna Lani Golf Course and
Clubhouse, South Kohala, Hawai'i**
LINKS Magazine, 'Best of Golf'
Award

1995 **Heidelberg Residential
Development, Taichung, Taiwan,
China**
Republic of China, High Quality
Architecture Award

1994 **Maui Arts & Cultural Center,
Kahului, Hawai'i**
American Institute of Architects
Honolulu Chapter, Award of Merit

1994 **Special Events Arena, University
of Hawai'i at Manoa, Honolulu,
Hawai'i**
American Society of Civil Engineers
Hawaii Section, Achievement Award

1994 **Hotel Conrad/Jupiters Casino
Arrivals Plaza Refurbishment,
Broadbeach, Queensland,
Australia**
Australian Institute of Landscape
Architects, Award of Merit

1994 **Sydney International Athletic and
Aquatic Centres, Homebush, New
South Wales, Australia**
Concrete Masonry Association of
Australia, Excellence Award

1994 **Hyatt Regency Kaua'i, Storm
Damage Assistance, Poipu, Hawai'i**
Consulting Engineers Council of
Hawaii, Honor Award

1994 **Kamehameha Industrial Center,
Honolulu, Hawai'i**
Consulting Engineers Council of
Hawaii, Honor Award

1994 **The Bluffs at Mauna Kea, South
Kohala, Hawai'i**
Gold Nugget Award, Award of Merit,
Residential Project of the Year

1994 **The Bluffs at Mauna Kea, South
Kohala, Hawai'i**
Gold Nugget Award, Best Condo or
Attached Home

1994 **1100 Alakea Plaza, Honolulu,
Hawai'i**
Hawaiian Cement, Concrete
Achievement Judges' Award

1994 **Waikapu Valley Country Club,
Wailuku, Hawai'i**
Hawaiian Cement, Concrete
Achievement Low-Rise Building
Award

1994 **Hotel Conrad/Jupiters Casino
Arrivals Plaza Refurbishment,
Broadbeach, Queensland,
Australia** [13]
Illuminating Engineering Society
of Australia & New Zealand,
Meritorious Lighting Award

1994 **Armata Court, Wattle Grove, New
South Wales, Australia**
Master Builders' Association of New
South Wales, Excellence in Housing
Awards, Best Public Housing

1994 **The Anchorage at Tweed Heads,
New South Wales, Australia**
Master Builders' Association of New
South Wales, Excellence in Housing
Award

1994 **MLC Centre, Sydney, Australia**
Master Builders' Association of New
South Wales, National Building &
Construction Award

1994 **Margate Foreshore Design
Competition, Margate Beach,
Queensland, Australia**
Redcliffe City Council, Design
Citation

1993 **Wo International Center, Punahou
School, Honolulu, Hawai'i**
American Institute of Architects
Honolulu Chapter, Design
Excellence Award

10

11

12

13

14

15

16

17

1993 **Bali Golf & Country Club, Nusa Dua, Bali, Indonesia**
American Society of Landscape Architects, Hawaii Chapter, Design Excellence Award

1993 **Ewa Beach International Golf Course and Country Club, Ewa Beach, Hawai'i**
American Society of Landscape Architects, Hawaii Chapter, Design Excellence Award

1993 **Safari Park Hotel, Nairobi, Kenya** [14]
American Society of Landscape Architects, Hawaii Chapter, Design Excellence Award

1993 **Pacific Place, Hong Kong, China**
British Association of Landscape Industries, National Landscape Award

1993 **Ke'ehi Lagoon Canoe Facility, Honolulu, Hawai'i**
Consulting Engineers Council of Hawaii, Honor Award

1993 **Hale Koa Hotel Pool & Luau Facility Renovation and Landscaping, Honolulu, Hawai'i**
Honolulu Magazine, Hawaii Renaissance Merit Award

1993 **Sydney International Athletic and Aquatic Centres, Homebush, New South Wales, Australia**
International Olympic Committee Award

1993 **The King's Shops, Waikoloa Beach Resort, South Kohala, Hawai'i**
National Commercial Builders Award

1993 **Anglican Retirement Village Hydrotherapy Centre, Castle Hill, New South Wales, Australia**
New South Wales Landscape Contractors Association, Excellence in Landscape Construction Award

1993 **The Anchorage at Tweed Heads, New South Wales, Australia**
New South Wales Landscape Contractors Association, Excellence in Landscape Construction Award, Multi-Housing

1992 **Bernice Pauahi Bishop Memorial Chapel & Heritage Center, Kamehameha Schools, Honolulu, Hawai'i** [15]
American Institute of Architects Honolulu Chapter, Design Excellence Award

1992 **Hyatt Regency Kaua'i, Poipu, Hawai'i**
American Institute of Architects Honolulu Chapter, Grand Award

1992 **Ewa Beach International Golf Course and Country Club, Ewa Beach, Hawai'i** [16]
Consulting Engineers Council of Hawaii, Honor Award

1992 **Mauna Lani Golf Course and Clubhouse, South Kohala, Hawai'i**
Golf Magazine, Gold Medal Award

1992 **Ilikai Hotel Nikko Landscape Renovations, Honolulu, Hawai'i**
Honolulu Magazine, Hawaii Renaissance Award

1992 **The Anchorage at Tweed Heads, New South Wales, Australia**
Master Builders' Association of New South Wales, Excellence in Housing Award

1991 **Linekona School, Honolulu, Hawai'i** [17]
American Institute of Architects Honolulu Chapter, Award of Merit

1991 **No. 1 Capitol District Building (formerly Hemmeter Corporate Offices), Honolulu, Hawai'i**
American Institute of Architects Honolulu Chapter, Award of Merit

1991 **Kohala Ranch Planned Residential Community, North Kohala, Hawai'i**
Consulting Engineers Council of Hawaii, Honor Award

1991 **Hawaii Prince Hotel Waikiki, Honolulu, Hawai'i**
Hawaii Concrete Building Award

1990 **Mauna Lani Resort, South Kohala, Hawai'i**
American Society of Civil Engineers, Hawaii Section, Merit Award

1990 **Mauna Lani Resort, South Kohala, Hawai'i**
Consulting Engineers Council of Hawaii, Honor Award

1990 **Mauna Kea Beach Hotel, South Kohala, Hawai'i**
Golf Magazine Gold Medal

1990 **Mauna Lani Golf Course and Clubhouse, South Kohala, Hawai'i**
Golf Magazine, Gold Medal Award

1989 **West Loch Estates Golf Course, Ewa Beach, Hawai'i**
American Institute of Architects, Hawaii Chapter, Award of Merit

1989 **Kauai Lagoons Resort, Lihu'e, Hawai'i** [18]
American Society of Civil Engineers, Hawaii Section, Merit Award

1989 **Ewa Water System Master Plan, Ewa Beach, Hawai'i**
Consulting Engineers Council of Hawaii, Honor Award

1988 **Kalakaua Avenue Safety and Beautification Project, Honolulu, Hawai'i**
City & County of Honolulu, Project of the Year

1988 **Kauai Lagoons Resort, Lihu'e, Hawai'i**
Consulting Engineers Council of Hawaii, Honor Award

1988 **Mauna Lani Golf Course and Clubhouse, South Kohala, Hawai'i**
Golf Magazine, Gold Medal Award

1988 **Hawaii State Capitol, Honolulu, Hawai'i**
State of Hawaii, Hawaiian Architectural Arts Award

1988 **Mauna Kea Beach Hotel Tennis Complex, South Kohala, Hawai'i**
Tennis Industry Magazine, Court of the Year

1988 **Mauna Lani Bay Hotel Tennis Complex, South Kohala, Hawai'i**
Tennis Industry Magazine, Court of the Year

1987 **Kalakaua Avenue Safety and Beautification Project, Honolulu, Hawai'i**
Aloha Magazine/University of Hawaii School of Travel Industry Management, Pacesetter Award

1987 **Aberdeen Marina Club, Hong Kong**
American Institute of Architects, Hawaii Chapter, Award of Merit

1987 **Glen Alpine, Campbelltown, New South Wales, Australia**
Australia Department of Housing/*Sun* Newspaper, 'Land Development' Award

1987 **'The Portico' at Mauna Olu Estates, Makaha, Hawai'i**
Building Industry Association of Hawaii/Honolulu Board of Realtors, Parade of Homes

1987 **Kalakaua Avenue Safety and Beautification Project, Honolulu, Hawai'i** [19]
Consulting Engineers Council of Hawaii, Honor Award

1987 **Mauna Kea Beach Hotel, South Kohala, Hawai'i**
Urban Land Institute (ULI), Award for Excellence

1986 **Mauna Lani Bay Resort and Bungalows, South Kohala, Hawai'i**
American Association of Nurserymen

1986 **Hilton Waikoloa Village, South Kohala, Hawai'i**
Consulting Engineers Council of Hawaii, Honor Award

1986 **The Anchorage at Tweed Heads, New South Wales, Australia** [20]
Master Builders' Association of New South Wales, Excellence in Housing Award

1985 **Shangri-La Hotel, Singapore**
American Society of Landscape Architects, Hawaii Chapter, Design Excellence Award

1985 **Outrigger Canoe Club Grounds Maintenance Program, Honolulu, Hawai'i**
American Society of Landscape Architects, Hawaii Chapter, Merit Award

1985 **Lalamilo Water System, South Kohala, Hawai'i**
Consulting Engineers Council of Hawaii, Honor Award

1984 **Mauna Lani Golf Course and Clubhouse, South Kohala, Hawai'i**
American Society of Landscape Architects, Hawaii Chapter, Merit Award

1984 **Moloka'i Water Systems Plan, Moloka'i, Hawai'i**
Consulting Engineers Council of Hawaii, Honor Award

1984 **St. John's Building Landscape, Hong Kong, China**
Hong Kong Institute of Architects

1983 **Punahou School Physical Education and Athletic Facilities, Honolulu, Hawai'i** [21]
Consulting Engineers Council of Hawaii, Honor Award

1983 **Tanjong Jara Beach Hotel and Rantau Abang Visitors Center, Kuala, Terengganu, Malaysia**
The Aga Khan Award for Architecture

1982 **The Anchorage at Tweed Heads, New South Wales, Australia**
American Society of Landscape Architects, Hawaii Chapter, Design Excellence Award

1982 **Royal Hawaiian Shopping Center, Honolulu, Hawai'i**
American Society of Landscape Architects, Hawaii Chapter, Merit Award

1982 **Kahuku Seafood Plantation Phase II, Kahuku, Hawai'i**
Consulting Engineers Council of Hawaii, Honor Award

1981 **Honolulu Program of Waste Energy Recovery (H-POWER) Environmental Impact Statement, Honolulu, Hawai'i**
American Consulting Engineers Council, National Award

18

19

20

21

22

23

24

1981 **Honolulu Program of Waste Energy Recovery (H-POWER) Environmental Impact Statement, Honolulu, Hawai'i**
Consulting Engineers Council of Hawaii, Honor Award

1980 **Tripler Army Medical Center Solar Energy Study, Honolulu, Hawai'i**
Consulting Engineers Council of Hawaii, Honor Award

1979 **Wai'ale'ale Hydropower Study, Kaua'i, Hawaii**
Consulting Engineers Council of Hawaii, Honor Award

1978 **Kapalua Resort Infrastructure Master Plan, Kapalua, Hawai'i** [22]
Consulting Engineers Council of Hawaii, Honor Award

1977 **Sydney Airport Centre, Sydney, Australia**
American Association of Nurserymen

1977 **Aliamanu Military Housing, Honolulu, Hawai'i**
Consulting Engineers Council of Hawaii, Honor Award

1976 **Wailea Resort, Wailea, Hawai'i** [23]
American Association of Nurserymen

1976 **Napilihau Residential Project, Napili, Hawai'i**
Consulting Engineers Council of Hawaii, Honor Award

1975 **Mauna Kea Beach Hotel, South Kohala, Hawai'i** [24]
American Association of Nurserymen

1975 **Kohala Coast Resort Region Plan, Hawai'i**
American Society of Landscape Architects, Hawaii Chapter, Merit Award

1975 **Taiwan Visitor Industry Program, Taiwan, China**
American Society of Landscape Architects, Hawaii Chapter, Merit Award

1975 **West Hawai'i Corridor Study, Hawai'i**
American Society of Landscape Architects, Hawaii Chapter, Merit Award

1975 **Ali'i Drive Realignment, Environmental Impact Statement and Design, Kailua-Kona, Hawai'i**
Consulting Engineers Council of Hawaii, Honor Award

1974 **Kona Surf Resort, Keauhou, Hawai'i**
American Association of Nurserymen

1974 **Kona Surf Resort, Keauhou, Hawai'i**
American Society of Landscape Architects, Hawaii Chapter, Merit Award

1974 **Haleakala National Park Water Improvement Study, Maui, Hawai'i**
Consulting Engineers Council of Hawaii, Honor Award

1973 **Kauai Surf Hotel Landscape, Lihu'e, Hawai'i**
American Association of Nurserymen

1972 **Kawaihae Village Development Plan, South Kohala, Hawai'i**
Consulting Engineers Council of Hawaii, Honor Award

1971 **Waialae-Iki Ridge Community Development Plan, Honolulu, Hawai'i**
Consulting Engineers Council of Hawaii, Honor Award

1970 **Kaiko'o Redevelopment Project, Hilo, Hawai'i**
Consulting Engineers Council of Hawaii, Honor Award

1969 **West Hawai'i Corridor Study, Hawai'i**
American Consulting Engineers Council, National Award

1969 **Dole Playground, Honolulu, Hawai'i**
American Institute of Architects, Hawaii Chapter, Award of Merit

1969 **West Hawai'i Corridor Study, Hawai'i**
Consulting Engineers Council of Hawaii, Honor Award

The many talented people shown below represent the heart of Belt Collins. It is their energy, their ideas and their follow-through that has created the Belt Collins of today. They represent a wonderful cross-section in age, gender and ethnicity of the regions where Belt Collins operates. To this great team we dedicate this book, which only shows a small portion of the more than 10,000 built projects they have created for our clients.

COLLEAGUES

Rohaina Adam
Rozita Adam
Lawrence Agena
Kerry Ahn
Aaron Akau
Dennis Alonzo
Azman Amir
Vorrarit Anantsorrarak
John Anderson
Loo Sing Ang
Karon Aoki
Vickie Asato
Chutima Aungatichart
Sakeson Aungsila
James Bell
Walter Billingsley
Christopher Bonilla
Stuart Brogan
Joel Burega
Raymond Cain
Michael Calleon
Victor Caparroso
Celso Caspe
Joseph Castillo
Rodolfo Castillo
Walter Castro
Rommel Centeno
Camille Chan
Ivan Chan
Janice Chan
Terence Chan
Tommy Chan
Tracy Chan
Willis Chan
Mabel Chang
Lulu Chen
Albert Cheng
Gary Cheng
Joann Cheng
Mandy Cheng
Sunshine Cheng
Sarah Cheung
Jessica Chiao
Lindsay Chong
Vincent Chow
Alex Chung
John Chung
Jolene Chung
Steven Chung
Tessa Chung
Jerry Coburn
Ireneo Comia
Christian Cruz
Robert Cunningham
Jane Dewell
Grant Donald
Chittsupha Don-an
Ian Duncan
Josie Evangelista
Janis Fedorowick
Yvonne Fernandez
Christine Flauta
Nancy Fok
Wyman Fong

Amy Foong
Benjamin Francisco
Douglas Froning
Lynn Fukuhara
Edwin Galicia
Michael Garris
Made Gede
Peter Geyer
Philip Guerrero
Anne Habedank
Somprasong Hachak
Abdul Halim
Sandy Hamura
Christian Harada
Edie Harakuni
Patricia Hayashi
Edean Hayashida
Robert Henson
Dawn Higa
Craig Hironaka
Willow Ho
Scott Hostetler
Aster Hu
Anthony Hui
Murray Hutchins
Ferdinand Inojosa
Royden Ishii
Satit Jakkaew
Unnop Jenkanpana
LaMarr Jones
Pasongjit Kaewdang
Penny Kamahiai
Gladys Kaneshiro
Alan Kato
Brian Kawamoto
Vanessa Kawamura
Carol Kazunaga
Brian Kellehar
Amy Kepilino
Allen Mark Kerton
YongGi Kim
Seksan Klomsungnoen
Cary Kondo
Andy Kong
Lilian Kong
Glen Koyama
Hilda Kunishige
Edwin Kuniyoshi
Alan Kutsunai
Alice Kwong
Calvin Lai
Sara Lai
Elaine Lam
Johnny Lam
Kim Cheong Lam
Wing Lam
Johnny Lau
Shirley Law
Teresa Law
Carrie Lee
Esther Lee
Gregory Lee
Jas Lee
Leland Lee

Steven Lee
Piyawan Leevairoj
Somwong Leevanijkul
Carolyn Len
Candy Leong
Shirley Leong
Jessica Leung
Vivian Leung
Caroline Li
William Li
Hui Onn Lim
Sheau Huay Lim
T. Y. Lim
Jesmond Lo
Angelic Loh
Onofre Lomboy
Darryl Lum
Claris Ma
Ruben Mallorca
Benny Man
Sirintira Maneesri
James Manibog
Anne Mapes
Carlos Mariano
Maura Mastriani
Lesley Matsumoto
Robin Matsunaga
Arnold Mcradu
Raoul Mendez
Daniel Miller
Lisa Minato
Edwin Miyashiro
Ken Mong
Muhd Dzaki Mustafi
Ranjani Nagaraj
Roy Nakagawa
Duanphen Netprasetkun
Marvin Ng
Patrick Ng
Veronica Ng
Daughn O'Neill
Gregg Onuma
Trina Onuma
Kiyomi Oyama
Cheryl Palesh
Roberto Pantaleon
Thomas Papandrew
John Parangat
Nelson Pascua
Renato Patricio
Roong-aroon Promvej
Tyler Puter
Edgar Quinabo
Nereo Racela
Benjamin Rasa
Lisa Reinke
Albert Rivera
Lawrence Robbins
Susan Sakai
Rommel San Diego
Nordin Sariman
Noranne Scott
Boonprakong Seedad
Carol Sham

Alan Shek
Lung Shek
Rodney Shiroma
Shing Shum
Lee Sichter
Stuart Soong
Suwat Srithong
Arlette St. Romain
Edward Stillinger
Christine Sung
Annabella Tabo-Nair
John Taira
Elizabeth Tajima
Francis Tam
Philip Tam
Florence Tan
Robin Tan
Veronica Tan
Christina Tang
Mark Tawara
Jason Teo
Teck Teo
Supasit Tepumnuaysakul
Michael Terry
Rushasri Tewinburanuwong
Tina Thian
Maverick Tin
Candy Tiong
Boon-anong Treenumitr
Claudia Tsang
Karen Tsoi
Nanthaporn Tuntipanichgool
Jirapong U-Bolsri
Susan Uejo
Richard Van Horn
Nipaporn Vibulchak
Danilo Victoria
Joseph Vierra, Jr.
Paul Wallrabenstein, Jr.
Kenneth Watanabe
Pontjo Widodo
Jason Wilson
Ali Wong
Jeannette Wong
Kelly Wong
Mei Lai Wong
Sofia Wong
Vanessa Wong
Yangi Wong
Augustine Woo
Esther Wu
Hsiu Ling Wu
Amy Yamakawa
Diane Yamamoto
William Yau
Sebastian Yeow
Avis Yeung
Gene Yong
Gary Yoshimura
Jon Young
Carson Yuen
Jimmy Yuen
(as of March 2003)

ACKNOWLEDGMENTS

In preparing a book that spans 50 years of projects from a firm like Belt Collins, there are individuals whose contributions are invaluable. Jim Bell, who originally joined Belt Collins in June 1953 as a summer intern and eventually rose to hold the firm's top leadership position for 30 years, was incredibly valuable for his institutional memory. Jim insisted on a balanced presentation of the firm's disciplines, and hopefully that has been achieved.

Other key participants in the senior management group were Tom Papandrew, whose guiding vision for the book was sorely needed all along the way, and Joe Vierra, who brought the engineering perspective to this effort. Legendary Ray Cain lent his sage advice on many of the book's projects. Everyone counted on Anne Mapes, head of Belt Collins Hawaii, to bring her great sense of the English language to the effort, and she did.

The management of Belt Collins offices in Asia and the Pacific added critical information and images to the effort, particularly Allen Kerton of the Singapore office and his staff member John Anderson, Anthony Hui and Peter Smulders of the Hong Kong office, and Somwong Leevanijkul of the Bangkok office. Lindsey Thorpe provided a lot of information about the firm's Australian projects.

Keen eyes are always necessary in preparing a book like this and Edean Hayashida and Cheryl Goody lent theirs over and over again. Pat Hayashi is a master at organizing and grading images, and without her sterling effort this book would not be what it is. Ron Goetz' gifted hands produced the sketches throughout the book.

An early participant in coordinating the book was a young marketing intern by the name of Andy Tamasese. Mark Tawara must be credited with bringing the idea for this book to life, and he was the marketing force behind the whole project.

David Cheever wrote the copy for the book.

Finally, heartfelt thanks go to Alessina Brooks and Paul Latham of Images Publishing who encouraged and cajoled us to the finish line.

PHOTOGRAPHY CREDITS

Belt Collins
All photographs except marked ones below

Tom Anthony
188 (3)

Bali InterContinental Resort
53; 60 (1); 61 (4); 63 (8)

Banyan Tree Resorts
71 (4); 213 (5)

Rob Brown
108 (4); 109 (8)

Ray Burgess / Sight Photographics
102 (1,2); 103 (3-5); 154 (2); 155 (3); 156 (5); 157 (7); 165 (1,2); 166 (3,4); 170 (2); 171 (3); 172 (4-6); 173 (7,8); 176 (2); 177 (5)

George Cadona
125 (7); 127 (12,14)

Castle & Cooke Properties, Inc.
121 (9)

Camera Hawaii
13; 14; 24 (2,3); 25 (5); 31; 34 (2); 35 (3); 36; 37; 39 (7,10); 40 (2); 42 (7); 49 (3); 106 (1); 108 (4,6); 109 (9); 120 (7); 121 (10); 176 (1); 210; 211; 216 (17); 217 (18, 21); 218 (22,24)

Romeo Collado
18 (1,2); 19 (3); 24 (4); 25 (6); 26 (3); 27 (5); 28 (9,10); 121 (10); 210

Ron Dahlquist
119 (3)

Dana Edmunds
186 (1); 187 (6)

Fairways Northwest Inc.
119 (4)

David Franzen
8; 80; 81 (2,3)

Michael French
22 (3)

Peter French
186 (2-4); 187 (5)

Ed Gross / The Image Group
41 (4); 44 (1); 45 (3); 47 (9); 48 (2); 51 (7); 117 (3)

Bill Hagstotz
144 (1)

Hawaii Infomart Project
32

Hayman Island Resort
56 (4)

David Heenan
54 (1,2); 57 (5)

Olivier Koning
11; 15 (2); 16 (5,6); 17 (9); 21 (2); 22 (5); 23 (8); 33; 38 (8); 41 (5); 43 (9); 46 (4,5); 47 (6,8); 48 (1); 109 (8); 115 (4); 116 (1,2); 117 (4,5); 118 (2); 120 (5); 123; 143 (5); 146 (2,3); 147 (4,5); 162 (1,3); 163 (4-6); 166 (1); 174 (1-3); 175 (4,5); 177 (3); 204 (1); 205 (3); 206 (5)

Laguna Phuket
76 (1); 133 (4-6); 135 (2,4); 136 (7); 138 (1); 139 (2,3)

Le Royal Meridien Baan Taling Ngam
58 (1,2); 59 (4)

Lend Lease
103 (4); 154 (1); 156 (6); 188 (1); 189 (5)

Irwin C. Malzman
145 (4,5)

Warren Marr
79; 94

Mauna Kea Properties, Inc.
27 (6); 39 (9)

Douglas Peebles
20 (1); 23 (7)

Palace of the Golden Horses
149 (4,5)

PT Freeport Indonesia
181 (6)

Queensland Department of Natural Resources & Mines
56 (3)

Raffles International
126 (9)

Kyle Rothenborg
158 (1,3); 159 (4); 160 (5-7); 161 (8,10)

The Royal Hawaiian
15 (3); 16 (4)

Joe Solem
28 (7)

Taman Dayu
192 (7)

Wailea Golf Resort, Inc.
112 (1,2); 113 (3,4); 218 (23)

Worldwide TV Productions
132 (2); 134 (1); 135 (3,5); 136 (6); 137 (8,9)

Wimberly Allison Tong & Goo (WATG)
64 (1,3); 65 (4,5)

Renderings

Ron Goetz
Endpapers; 60; 62; 134; 136; 137

Belt Collins
44 (2); 114 (1); 126 (10); 132 (3); 194; 195; 196

INDEX

The information and illustrations in this publication has been prepared and supplied by Belt Collins. While all reasonable efforts have been made to ensure accuracy, the publishers do not, under any circumstances, accept responsibility for errors, omissions and representations express or implied.